LIGHTING
DESIGN & INSTALLATION

*Techniques & Projects for
Lighting Your Home and Landscape*

CREATIVE
PUBLISHING
international

CHANHASSEN, MINNESOTA

www.creativepub.com

D1534339

Creative Publishing international, Inc.
18705 Lake Drive East
Chanhassen, Minnesota 55317
1-800-328-3895
www.creativepub.com

President/CEO: Michael Eleftheriou
Vice President/Publisher: Linda Ball
Vice President/Retail Sales & Marketing:
  Kevin Haas

Executive Editor: Bryan Trandem
Creative Director: Tim Himsel
Managing Editor: Michelle Skudlarek
Editorial Director: Jerri Farris

Lead Writer: Andrew Karre
Copy Editor: Karen Ruth
Proofreader: Anne Todd
Senior Art Director: David Schelitzche
Mac Designer: Jon Simpson
Illustrators: David Schelitzche,
  Jon Simpson
Project Managers: Julie Caruso,
  Tracy Stanley
Photo Researcher: Julie Caruso
Studio Services Manager:
  Jeanette Moss McCurdy
Photographer: Tate Carlson
Technical Photo Editor: Randy Austin
Photo Stylists: Julie Caruso,
  Joanne Wawra
Scene Shop Carpenter: Randy Austin
Director, Production Services &
  Photography: Kim Gerber
Production Manager: Stasia Dorn

Cover photo courtesy of Hubbardton Forge®

Library of Congress
Cataloging-in-Publication Data

Lighting design & installation: techniques &
projects for lighting your home and landscape.
    p. cm.
  ISBN 1-58923-095-7 (soft cover)
  1. Lighting.
  TH7703.L54 2003
  621.32--dc21

2003046226

CONTENTS

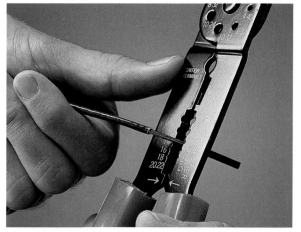

INTRODUCTION

Light is the first of painters. There is no object so foul that intense light will not make it beautiful.

–Ralph Waldo Emerson

Light is much more than just a utility. Light can affect us and the way we sense the world more than any other feature in our homes—it's something worth being particular about.

Being particular is one thing, but understanding what we want from this elusive thing called light is a little more difficult to articulate. We want our homes to look good and we want to feel comfortable in them, and for that we need good light, but what exactly is good light and how do we get it? This book offers some answers.

Creating good lighting is not just a matter of having "enough" light or of getting attractive fixtures and the right switches. Good lighting is ultimately a matter of achieving a desired look and feel. Light can shape our moods. It can soothe the mind and invigorate the body. Light, in all of its manifestations, has the power not only to illuminate what we see, but influence *how* we see it, even to make it beautiful. More than anything else, good lighting comes from being able to choose exactly how we want light to influence the way a space looks and feels.

Excellence doesn't have to be a luxury item, and good lighting is not necessarily expensive. Understanding how light works and carefully planning for intended effects will help you light your home effectively and beautifully on almost any budget. In this book you'll find the information you need to understand the choices available to you, and the guidance to help you create a plan. You'll also find clear, step-by-step instructions for more than a dozen lighting projects, should you choose to install new lighting yourself. Most importantly, there are over a hundred color photos to light your own creative fires.

When you make the decision to improve the light in your home, you not only decide to make everyday tasks easier and more comfortable, you choose to show your home at its best and emphasize the details that make it your own. Be creative and have fun.

UNDERSTANDING LIGHT

There's a certain Slant of light,

–Emily Dickinson

I t's easy to tell when the light is right. Intuition guides you; you look around the room and everything just feels right. You don't notice the lights, but you are drawn in by the feeling light creates. Sometimes creating this feeling is as easy as turning down the lamps and lighting a few candles. Suddenly the lighting and the mood harmonize. The light is good, and everything is beautiful and balanced.

If the light isn't right, you know it immediately. Bad light clashes with objects rather than enhances them. At its worst, it makes us feel uncomfortable and makes work harder. The lighting in most homes is rarely completely wrong, but it is often uncomfortable or poorly designed and in need of improvement.

When it comes to selecting and placing new lights, though, it's easy to be overwhelmed by the options. Gut feelings don't always help. You won't find bulbs rated "for a bright, airy kitchen with stainless steel countertops" or fixtures labeled "for a cozy study with dark paneled walls." Instead, lightbulbs and fixtures speak their own language—watts, lumens, "full spectrum," and so on—which makes for a challenge when trying to turn intuition into a practical plan. What you need is objective information.

The place to start is at the source. Learning the language of lightbulbs and a bit of the science behind them will allow you to understand, for instance, why your kitchen lights make everything look green or why a new reading lamp seems so harsh. Getting to know lightbulbs is the first step in turning imagination into a design and a design into reality. The chapter that follows will put you well on your way to understanding the hundreds of bulbs at the typical home improvement center.

LIGHTBULBS

Lightbulbs—or lamps, as lighting designers call them—are simple devices, and we tend to take them for granted, often buying them indiscriminately and in large quantities. Almost everyone has a drawer or cupboard full of 60-watt incandescent bulbs. But replacing a lightbulb, no matter how many people it takes, isn't as simple as it might seem. Every type of lightbulb has different strengths and weaknesses, and there is no such thing as an all-purpose bulb. Matching a bulb's qualities to the space or task it will illuminate can be the easiest (and least expensive) way to upgrade a lighting design.

The first step in choosing bulbs is understanding the basic types and how they work. We get our artificial light mainly from lightbulbs of two familiar types: incandescent and fluorescent. Both types create light by running electrical current through some sort of medium that glows when energized. In the case of the standard incandescent bulb, the medium is a thin metal filament (typically made of tungsten) in a bulb filled with inert gas. The filament glows because it's hot, but since the bulb contains no oxygen, it doesn't flame. The design is not significantly different from Thomas Edison's. Today's halogen and xenon bulbs are also incandescent bulbs, but are filled with halogen or xenon gas, which affects the intensity, color qualities, and efficiency of the light.

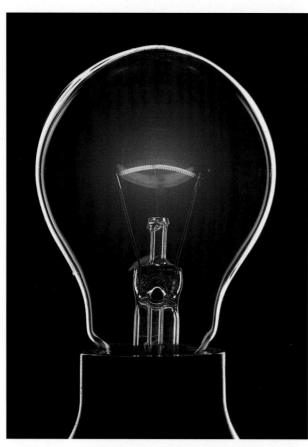

The design of the incandescent lightbulb has changed surprisingly little since Edison invented it over a century ago. The tungsten filament glows as electrical current passes through it.

Fluorescent lights use ballasts, which send specific voltage through vapor in the tube. The vapor causes an ultraviolet arc that causes the coating on the tube to glow brightly.

Fluorescent bulbs are a bit more complicated than incandescents but, whether standard tubes or the newer CFL type (compact fluorescent lamp), all fluorescent bulbs generally work the same way. Fluorescent bulbs are mercury vapor-filled chambers. The inside of the bulb is coated with phosphors that fluoresce (glow) when current flowing through the vapor causes an ultraviolet arc. To create a consistent arc and thus a consistent light, the electrical current must be regulated by a device called a ballast, which is generally built into fluorescent lamps and fixtures (see information below).

A third type of bulb, similar to fluorescents, is the *high intensity discharge* or HID lamp.

BALLASTS

All fluorescent bulbs must have ballasts to regulate the flow of current through the tube. Not all ballasts are the same, though, and this seemingly innocuous bunch of wires can ruin an otherwise good fixture. Simple magnetic ballasts, such as those found on old fluorescent fixtures or on newer inexpensive ones, are the source of the irritating buzzing so many people associate with fluorescent tubes. They also can shorten the life of bulbs and cause them to flicker. Newer electronic ballasts have a much more rapid cycle and do not produce a detectable hum. They are available at home improvement centers for retrofitting on most fluorescent fixtures and can be a very easy way to upgrade an older fixture. Ballasts are also available that will allow you to dim some kinds of fluorescent fixtures, something that isn't possible with magnetic ballasts.

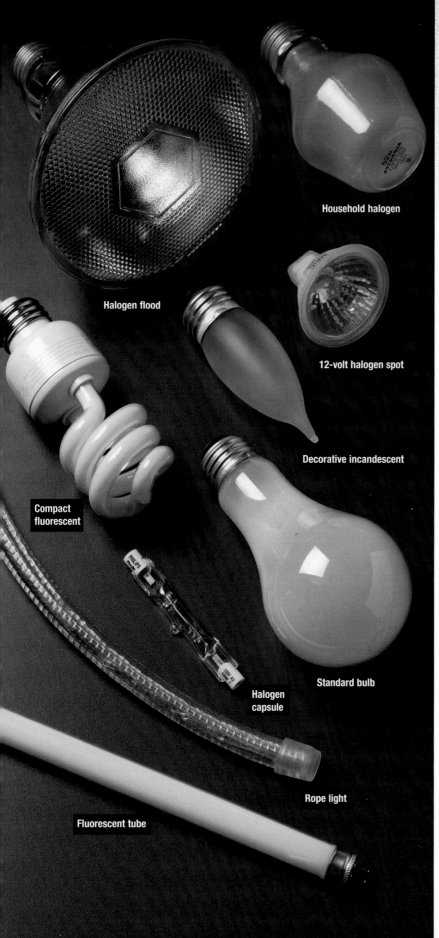

Household halogen

Halogen flood

12-volt halogen spot

Decorative incandescent

Compact fluorescent

Standard bulb

Halogen capsule

Fluorescent tube

Rope light

These bulbs are very energy efficient and very bright, but they have long start-up times, must be left on for long periods of time, and require special ballasts, so HID lamps are found in almost all parking lot lights and streetlights but in very few homes or yards.

Household incandescent and fluorescent bulbs are available in a huge variety of styles for indoor and outdoor use. Individual bulbs vary from manufacturer to manufacturer and each has strengths and weaknesses. New bulbs with new features are introduced regularly. A good lighting store is indispensible for providing information on what bulbs are available for your needs.

The rest of this chapter will focus on some of the science that separates a good lightbulb from a bad one and on how you can tell the difference.

Picking the right lightbulbs is easy and a good way to improve your home's lighting—if you know a little about the differences between the types.

COLOR TEMPERATURE

One of the most puzzling scientific terms in the lighting lexicon is *color temperature*. But it is the first one worth knowing because it can have the greatest positive effect on the bulb choices you make. Color temperature has nothing to do with how hot or cold our skin feels but how warm or cool colors and light look. Technically, color temperature is the temperature on the Kelvin (K) scale at which a theoretical perfect conductor would glow a certain color. That is, if you ran an electrical current through this fictitious filament and it heated to 2,000 Kelvin (3,140 degrees Fahrenheit), it would glow an orangish yellow. Just to make things confusing, though, the scale is inverted so that the higher the number and temperature, the cooler the color. A "cool" color, like blue, actually has a very high color temperature of around 7,000 Kelvin—more than three times hotter than a "warm" color like orange. Think about the color of a relatively cool candle flame compared to that of the much hotter blue flame of a gas stove and this will make sense.

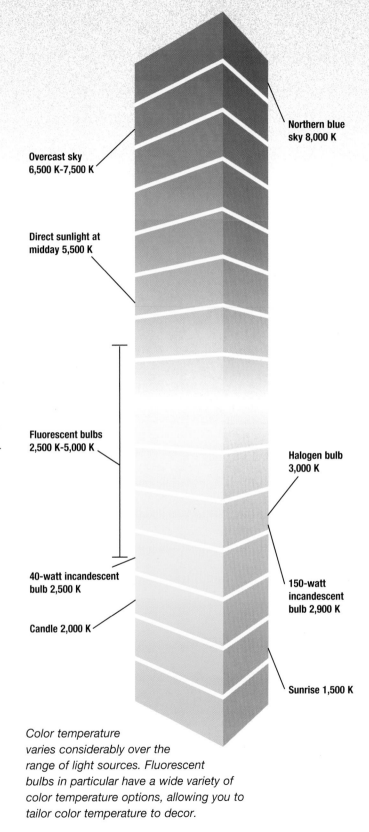

Northern blue sky 8,000 K

Overcast sky 6,500 K-7,500 K

Direct sunlight at midday 5,500 K

Fluorescent bulbs 2,500 K-5,000 K

Halogen bulb 3,000 K

40-watt incandescent bulb 2,500 K

150-watt incandescent bulb 2,900 K

Candle 2,000 K

Sunrise 1,500 K

Color temperature varies considerably over the range of light sources. Fluorescent bulbs in particular have a wide variety of color temperature options, allowing you to tailor color temperature to decor.

Differences in color temperature are visible. The fluorescent fixture in the industrial-look kitchen on the left has a color temperature of around 5,000 K, which harmonizes readily with the cold, hard metal and brick surfaces. The much warmer light—around 2,500 K— of the incandescent lamp on the right suits the warm muted tones and soft textures of this living room.

What all this means is that the color temperature scale is a consistent way to talk about the "warmth" or "coolness" of color, both for pigment and for light. Coordinating the relative warmth or coolness of colors in paints and fabrics is a familiar principle in decorating—you can generally feel when a warm color is clashing with a cool one or when the color is wrong for the mood. The principle extends to lighting. If the light in a room seems a little too cool and hard or warm and soft, part of the problem is probably a poor color temperature match between light and the surfaces it's illuminating.

The metals and gases used in lightbulbs are what give them unique color temperature values. The chart on page 11 gives the range of color temperatures and each common bulb type's place on it. Lighting specialty stores should be able to give you information about the color temperatures of specific brands and models if the bulb's packaging does not.

Color temperature applies to all light sources, not just lightbulbs. It's interesting to note that candlelight lies at the low end of the scale, explaining our sense that candlelight is somehow "warm." Some low-wattage incandescent bulbs have values very near to candlelight and thus seem similarly warm. Halogen bulbs, which have become popular in reading and desk lamps, have a noticeably higher temperature and generally produce cooler light. It is also worth noting that the much-maligned fluorescent tube—once exclusively a source of very cool, hard light—is widely available in models with a much lower color temperature (below 3,000 K), making their efficient and convenient light a good option for all sorts of rooms and decors.

While replacing all the lightbulbs in your living room with 40-watt incandescent bulbs will not give you the exact effect of candlelight, paying attention to color temperatures can pay dividends. Aside from what a room's coloring dictates, you probably have a sense for whether you want a warm- or cool-feeling light, and if you pick lightbulbs by color temperature, you can satisfy that need. For instance, a low-wattage standard incandescent bulb in a reading lamp by a favorite chair will create a gentle pool of light far warmer and perhaps more comfortable than the cool, bright light of the halogen bulbs that come standard in many new reading lamps. The reason is largely a difference in color temperature and bulb type. In general, choosing bulbs with attention to color temperatures can help harmonize the light with a decor or a mood.

COLOR RENDERING

Color temperature is a good way to understand the sense of warmth or coolness a light source gives, but there is another measure that also plays an important role in the way you perceive light and how it affects the color of the things it illuminates. Color rendering refers to a lightbulb's ability to show color accurately—to show red reds and truly white whites. You know a little about the different abilities of light types to render color if

Bulb types & color rendering

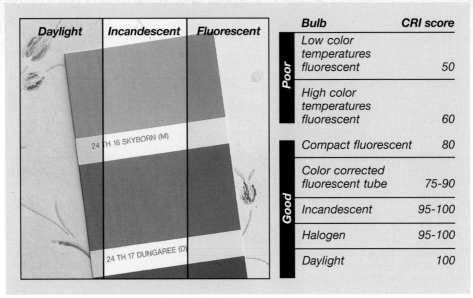

	Bulb	CRI score
Poor	Low color temperatures fluorescent	50
	High color temperatures fluorescent	60
Good	Compact fluorescent	80
	Color corrected fluorescent tube	75-90
	Incandescent	95-100
	Halogen	95-100
	Daylight	100

Good color rendering is helpful for showing color details in decor and for making close work easier. Look for bulbs with CRI scores of 75 or better. Bulbs with both warm and very cool color temperatures are available with high CRI scores.

you've ever held two socks to a window to tell a black sock from a blue one. Some lights just show color better than others, and the reason is in the light itself.

All light, no matter what color it appears to our eyes, contains a range of color from red through violet, a range known as the *visible light spectrum*. Pure white light contains an even distribution of all these colors and, as a result, renders color faithfully. Midday sunlight, for example, has this even distribution, which is why people go to the window to get a good sense of color. But not all light is truly white. Some artificial light sources, due to properties of their filaments and gases, produce more light at a certain wavelength and so have an excess of that color. This excess causes them to distort other colors. Older fluorescent tubes, for instance, produce a well-known excess of green and yellow. This means that when light from such a fluorescent tube strikes a surface, more green and yellow light reflects back, giving everything a slightly green cast.

Scientists have developed the *color rendering index* or CRI for ranking lightbulbs' color rendering properties. While manufacturers rarely put this value on lightbulb packaging, lightbulbs tend to fall into standard ranges on the CRI. "Full spectrum" incandescent

Distribution of color in forms of light

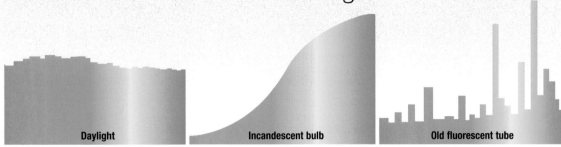

Daylight   Incandescent bulb   Old fluorescent tube

If you ever thought things looked a little green or yellow under some old fluorescent lights, these spectrographs should confirm your intuition. The excess of green light is quite extreme.

lightbulbs are one exception to this (see below). The chart on page 14 shows the CRI scores for most common bulb types.

Manufacturers have made progress in correcting fluorescent tubes' poor rendering, and color-corrected fluorescent bulbs—called *rare-earth* or *triphosphor* fluorescents—are now available.

Bulbs with exceptionally high CRI values are prized by painters and curators of art galleries, but are also appropriate for display lighting in homes. Specialty lighting stores can provide information about individual brands and models and can steer you toward bulbs with very high values—which are good upgrades for kitchens, laundry rooms, and other places where color discrimination is important.

"FULL SPECTRUM"

Full spectrum incandescent and fluorescent light bulbs have become widely available in the past few years. They create light the same way as standard incandescents or fluorescents, but, for quite a bit more money, these corrected bulbs promise a full complement of color, correcting the spikes that exist in standard incandescents or fluorescents. They accomplish this by using special coatings on the bulb, which filter out a certain amount of the excess light of a particular color. And while the color correction benefits of full spectrum light are quite true, it seems that the manufacturers are giving consumers the impression that full spectrum bulbs provide health benefits. This is not the case. While these bulbs arguably provide light that is more comfortable for the eyes than an uncorrected bulb and may, as a result, reduce eyestrain, there are no demonstrated physiological benefits. Light does play a role in physical and psychological health (see pages 18-19 for more on the benefits of natural light), but no full spectrum bulb used for general lighting provides light at the intensity necessary for any health benefits.

EFFICIENCY

Two numbers you will always find on a bulb package are *watts* and *lumens*. A bulb's wattage is a measure of power consumption, a measure used for all electrical devices. Lumens is a less familiar measurement of the amount of light emitted by the bulb in terms of volume—essentially it tells you how much space a lightbulb could illuminate. A single lumen is defined as the area illuminated by a single candle.

Commercial lighting designers make very precise calculations to determine the number of lumens needed to meet the illumination needs of a room, but these calculations have little practical value for homeowners. The most interesting information to be had is *efficacy*, a measure of a bulb's efficiency.

The most efficient bulb is one that produces the greatest number of lumens using the fewest watts—it's the lighting equivalent of miles per gallon. To make this a truly useful measurement, you should also consider a third number: longevity, the average number of operating hours a bulb will last. Efficacy has improved greatly since the invention of the lightbulb. Edison's first bulb produced a paltry .6 lumens per watt whereas a modern fluorescent is easily 100 times more efficient.

Efficacy is the driving force behind the use of fluorescent bulbs. Whatever their drawbacks, they have always been more efficient than standard incandescents by a wide margin—roughly the equivalent of comparing a 1950s Buick to a modern gas-electric hybrid car. In order to encourage residential use of these efficient bulbs, manufacturers have improved the color temperature and color rendering of fluorescents and developed ballasts that don't buzz or flicker. Adding concealed high-quality fluorescent tubes above cabinets (see page 82), behind molding (see page 84), or in custom-built ceiling boxes (see page 80), is an efficient and stylish alternative to using incandescent bulbs.

Manufacturers have also developed compact fluorescent lamps (CFLs), fluorescent bulbs meant to work in lamps and fixtures originally designed for incandescent bulbs. Not only are CFLs more efficient than the incandescents they replace—a 25 watt CFL can replace a 60 watt incandescent—but they last as much as ten times longer. They cost more initially but pay for themselves once in use.

Fiber optics & LEDs

Fiber optic lighting has been widely used in commercial and entertainment lighting for some time and is now beginning to make inroads into homes and residential landscaping. Fiber optic light is light carried along specially manufactured glass or plastic fibers—think of them as very efficient, thin, flexible light conducting tubes. A light generator—a box with a very bright lightbulb—feeds light into one end of the tubes. The tubes, which carry no current and do not get hot, can be routed through walls, into ceilings, through landscaping, or under water, and can carry light to places electricity can't safely go. The end of a tube can be fitted into a light fixture to direct the light once it leaves the tube. Filters and shades can control the quality of the visible light. The whole fiber can also be a fixture itself—much like a neon tube—if its length is left transparent and exposed.

Thin fiber optic strands can carry light where electric lights can't go.

There are many advantages to fiber optic lighting, from aesthetics to safety, but relatively few homes use it for anything other than decorative lighting. Light generators and high-quality fibers are expensive and using them to replace traditional light sources requires rethinking the way a house is wired. But the benefits of having all light emanate from a single remote source without the need for wiring are great. In the near future, fiber optics will very likely begin to replace many types of traditional electrical lighting, particularly in landscapes.

Light-emitting diodes (LEDs) are another light source making inroads into residences. LEDs are basically tiny light emitting microchips, and they are already common in electronic devices, cars, stoplights, and outdoor signs.

LEDs promise incredible flexibility and efficiency. Designers can program them to produce light of any color temperature and to have perfect CRI scores. They already far outlast even the most long-lived lightbulbs, use much less energy, and generate almost no heat. They even promise to be cheaper, once they are produced on a large scale. LEDs may be to lightbulbs what lightbulbs once were to gas lamps.

NATURAL LIGHT

Natural light is the primary light source in most rooms for much of the day, and some of the most profound improvements to a room's lighting can be made by working with available natural light. In the chapters that follow, you'll find several suggestions and techniques for maximizing daylight in your home. Daylight has some unique properties worth looking at in more detail, though.

Light from the sun is dynamic in ways that no artificial light source can be. As the sun moves across the sky, its characteristics and effects on you and your house change.

The unique properties of natural light play an important role in human health and well being.

Northern sunlight is markedly different from southern sunlight in terms of color temperature, color rendering, and how much heat it radiates. The earth's atmosphere acts like a coating on a bulb, deflecting certain parts of the sun's rays and admitting others as the angle of the sun rises and falls. Light from a northern clear blue sky is the coolest of all light, and provides a sense of clarity and sharpness along with excellent color rendering.

Sunlight is also intensely bright in a way not approached by any artificial light and this means that, beyond the aesthetic beauty of sunlight, it can have significant effects on human health. The difference in lumens between natural light and most artificial sources is on the order of the difference between a fire hose and a squirt gun. The sheer volume of light our eyes and skin receive when we are in sunlight is part of what affects our health. The dangers posed by the ultraviolet portion of sunlight on skin are well known and have been for some time, but only recently have scientists begun to make connections between the intense light from the sun and human biological cycles. The most interesting research—and the most significantly misunderstood—has been on Seasonal Affective Disorder (see below).

SEASONAL AFFECTIVE DISORDER

Though the clinical definition of Seasonal Affective Disorder (SAD) is somewhat controversial, SAD is essentially a winter-time depression caused by a biochemical imbalance in the body. This imbalance is associated with the diminished amount of light during the shorter days of winter. SAD afflicts millions, causing seasonal depression and drastically diminishing quality of life during the winter months.

Lighting has begun to play a peripheral role in treatment. Studies have shown that regular, prolonged exposure to light at daylight-like intensities (many hundreds of times greater than normal artificial levels) during periods of SAD-related depression can have a significant effect on symptoms. Special lamps fitted with high-intensity discharge bulbs are often prescribed for SAD patients. SAD sufferers spend a certain period of time every day near enough to the lamp that it is visible in their peripheral vision. Studies have shown some promising results from such treatments.

Contrary to some manufacturers advertising claims, intensity matters much more than the color spectrum of the light when it comes to treating SAD. No residential lighting product, bulb or fixture, can appropriately be used as a treatment for SAD. Doctors, not light-bulb manufacturers, treat SAD.

DESIGNING WITH LIGHT

Uniform lighting—the sweetheart of lighting engineers—serves no useful purpose whatsoever. In fact, it destroys the social nature of space and makes people feel disoriented and unbounded.

–Architect Christopher Alexander and colleagues, *A Pattern Language*

Understanding the light around you is a huge step toward creating good lighting. But there's more to lighting than just the light itself. Some of the words we use to describe a truly well-lit room, words like "cozy" or "intimate," don't describe qualities of the light itself in the way words like "warm" or "soft" do, but rather describe how light works with and in a space. To think of it another way, consider candlelight again. The beauty of a candlelit table for two is partially in the warm, flickering light unique to candles. But place the candle somewhere other than in the middle of the table, and the effect is different, the mood, changed.

It's no surprise that where fixtures are placed and how they aim light are critical—everyone has moved a lamp to get "better" light. The candle example tells us more than that, though. A table for two—whether in an apartment or a large restaurant—is its own space within the room. Every element emphasizes this, especially the light. The candle's dim light makes the diners lean in toward the candle and each other, while making everything else seem farther away. The pool of light from the candle creates a space.

It's important to create these spaces within all our rooms. As rooms get larger and houses become more open, we need to spend more time making them fit us. Light is one of the best tools we have for creating and defining these spaces.

To this end, experts divide light sources into four basic layers: **task**, **accent**, **ambient** and **decorative**. They have a repertoire of ways to use these layers to create and define spaces. This chapter will show you how to use these layers. The last half of the chapter also contains helpful advice on lighting surfaces, working with daylight, and on fixture and switch types.

21

TASK LIGHTING

Task lighting is the lighting layer you count on to make tasks and activities from reading to cooking easier and more pleasant. But good task lighting is more than having light sources bright enough to see what you're doing. Tasks and activities help define spaces within rooms, and good task lighting—from a variety of sources—defines and emphasizes these spaces while it makes working in them easier. When they are properly in place, you don't switch on task lights as much as you switch on task spaces.

A reading lamp by a chair is a task light, defining an important space within the room. If you walked into a perfectly evenly lit room with a comfortable chair placed at its center, you would probably find the space uninviting—too large for a task as personal and small as reading. We often don't feel comfortable in spaces that don't match the scale of our activities. A room with low background lighting and a warm pool of light from a lamp next to a chair, however, matches the scale of the activity with a similarly scaled space. You can feel comfortable curling up in such a space with a book and a cup of tea.

Look at any room in your home and you will probably be able to identify many specific spaces that would benefit from their own light sources. When builders build homes, they cannot predict how these spaces will evolve, so rooms often have just one or two sources of general lighting. The first step in improving the lighting in such a room is spreading the light over many sources to match how you use the room. By spreading light over several light sources associated with specific spaces, task lighting becomes more effective and more direct.

Even cavernous rooms like library reading rooms can be divided into human-sized spaces. Reading lamps provide a pool of light for each reading space.

Right: The combination of the contrasting block of color on the wall and gentle light from the shaded pendant create an inviting dining space within the kitchen. Below: Sconces on either side of a mirror make an ideal space for grooming.

Once you've brought the light source to the space, you have more control and flexibility. You can, for instance, use two counterbalancing sources to light a space. Designers call this cross lighting, and it's effective in all sorts of situations where shadow is a problem. Consider the bathroom mirror, where often a single light above the mirror is the only source of task lighting. Light from this single source won't illuminate the spaces below your eyebrows or cheekbones—you'll appear tired. If fixtures direct light in from the sides, however, any shadows cast by one light will be canceled by the other. Eliminating shadow is important, but unless your task is coercing confessions from suspects, adding glare isn't desirable. Think about your own line of sight in a space. You want to see the light, but not the light source.

One other consideration when choosing task lighting is the quality of the light—the color temperature and color rendering. Cool bulbs with high color rendering index scores are obvious choices for close tasks like sewing or cooking. When a sense of comfort and closeness is important, though—such as with a reading lamp—it may well be

worthwhile to sacrifice a little color rendering for a softer light to match the mood of the space.

With a good task lighting layer in place, you can begin adding details with accent lighting.

DIVIDE AND CONQUER: TASK LIGHTING IN THE KITCHEN

Task lighting is very important in kitchens, but many kitchens were built with most of their light concentrated in a single very bright central fixture. Lighting the middle of the room and the ceiling isn't all that important, but getting light to the countertops, sink, and other prep and eating areas is. Ideally, all of these spaces are best served by individual light sources.

Take the light from the glaring central fixture and put it to better use by dividing it up among the spaces in the kitchen. Put a recessed light or track lights over the sink and it will stay bright and shadowless even after the sun goes down. Add pendants or spots over an island and you brighten up valuable work and eating space. Add strip lights to the underside of the cabinets, and you shorten the distance light has to travel and reduce the number of objects casting shadows. Put a pendant with a chrome-bottom bulb over the breakfast table and you get a softly lit eating space.

The kitchen won't be any less bright, but there will be fewer shadows, less glare, and making and eating a meal will be easier and more relaxing.

ACCENT LIGHTING

If task lighting defines spaces, then accent lighting presents the various details of those spaces. The accent layer is another tool we can use to organize the spaces we live in and show off the beautiful objects in our lives.

We all decorate rooms with things that are important to us and with things we simply find beautiful. This is how we make spaces our own. You can take personalization to another level, though, by organizing and emphasizing objects with accent lighting—just as you create and define space with task lighting. A room with nothing but even, general light says everything it has to say at once, but careful accent lighting subtly presents your personality and style, emphasizing some things while de-emphasizing others. Accent lighting guides your eye and draws you into a room.

Accent lighting at its simplest is no more than a spotlight on an object. This is how museums illuminate art. The goal is bright light that shows every facet of the piece. Accent lighting in our homes may occasionally fall into this category—lighting a paint-

ing, for instance—but more often, accent lighting needs to be less direct or more exciting. So, rather than think like a museum curator, think like a painter. In art, you rarely find lighting that reveals everything. Great painters use light to compose space and to create moods—to hide as much as they show. Subjects are lit with an eye to the way light communicates underlying emotion, not just information. Free your imagination when it comes to placing accent lighting. Forget about showing

A recessed spotlight inconspicuously calls attention to this minimalist mantle.

Good accent lighting leaves something unsaid. A gentle beam of light just grazes this vase, creating a pleasing contrast between light and shade.

things clearly; instead think of withholding something with a well-placed beam of light. Highlight the tension between light and shadow. Think about what isn't illuminated. When you light objects with the intention of concealing as well as revealing, light will draw people to the object by leaving something to the imagination—and that's what you want from accent lighting in your rooms.

Tight beams of light from small spotlights are ideal for this sort of accent lighting. Direct light from below for bold, dramatic shadows. Light smaller objects on a shelf or mantel from the side to bring out large shadows. Create a vertical column of light by directing a beam down from above.

The things you accent need not be art objects at all—they can be architectural details. A finely finished wall or a ceiling with particularly beautiful detailing deserves accent lighting. Use a spotlight to accent a mural or faux finishing on a wall.

Objects and details take center stage with accent lighting, so fixtures can be inconspicuous. Part of the beauty of accent lighting, in fact, is that the fixtures needn't be fancy or expensive. In many cases, you don't even want to see them. Tiny and fairly inexpensive low-voltage recessed fixtures are perfect for ceilings and cabinets. Simple, cheap floor and table lamps and clip-on lights can be flexible tools for getting great accent effects.

Accent lights can also become part of an arrangement. A beautiful table lamp with a shade that complements the objects will create a soft pool of light and ample shadows while unobtrusively blending in with the rest of the display. Accent lights need not be bright—in fact, they can even be candles. What they must do, though, is draw the eye.

Another way to ensure that illumination blends with the illuminated is to pay attention to the quality of light you're using. Color rendering and color temperature are, of course, crucial to casting anything in a good light, but especially so for colorful or highly textured objects. A softly colored tapestry, for example, is a great candidate for display, but choosing the right bulb is worth some care. A cool halogen bulb with a near perfect color rendering index score will render its colors vividly, but you may find the contrast between the cool hardness of a halogen light and the soft warmth of the tapestry jarring. A far better choice is a softer, warmer frosted incandescent bulb. Even if the bulb's color rendering is slightly less accurate, the light will be more diffuse and will blend better with the colors of the fabric. Be sure any light you use to accent fabric or paper is UV filtered to avoid damaging the fibers.

Accent lighting also deserves attention for another, quite practical purpose: the more light you provide with accent lighting, the brighter you'll be able to make a room in general, and so you'll need fewer dedicated ambient fixtures. Once the task and accent lighting are in place, though, you may find you still need to add another layer of light to some rooms—which brings us to ambient lighting.

Above: Accent lights recessed in the ceiling rake this wall with light, highlighting the wall hanging and showing the dramatic texture of the wall. Right: A lamp with an opaque shade surrounds the objects below it with light.

AMBIENT LIGHTING

Ambient lighting is the diffuse light that illuminates a room from several sources and sets the minimum level of lighting. It needs to be considered last because you won't be sure how much dedicated ambient lighting you'll need until you have planned for the task and accent layers. Once in place though, the ambient layer provides a background, gently lighting areas not illuminated by specific task and accent lights. Looking from a bright space like the page of a book under a reading lamp into a dim, unlit room forces your eyes to adjust. Ambient light sources minimize this contrast and make a room more comfortable by producing just enough light to brighten the room without obscuring the spaces created by task and accent lights.

Artificial ambient light is most effective when it mimics daylight. Daylight is, after all, the primary source of ambient illumination for most of the day. Daylight has its own special character, though. In most rooms, light from the sun doesn't come through windows and skylights directly. It filters through clouds, reflects off the ground, and is generally diffused and softened before it arrives in a room. You look at a window and see light, but not the sun. In fact, in a room where sunlight is very intense, we often soften it with blinds or translucent curtains. We want our ambient light unfocused.

For artificial ambient lighting, follow daylight's example. Make it a rule that no ambient light will arrive at the eye without first

A combination of a cove lighting and spots directed at the ceiling brightens the boundaries of this room, providing comfortable, reflected ambient light.

reflecting off of another surface. This is easy in small rooms. "Extra" light from task and accent lighting reflects around the room and generally provides enough ambient light. In larger rooms, or in any room where a bit more background light is in order, position ambient sources to add to this extra reflected light. Torchieres—floor lamps that direct light up—placed in corners are a good choice. Ceiling fixtures and wall sconces that direct all of their light back to the ceiling or wall provide excellent reflected ambient light. Recessed lights designed to use chrome-bottom bulbs and reflectors can also provide inconspicuous reflected light. The most elegant solution, though, is to use several concealed sources of light. Fixtures can be hidden in architectural coves, behind trim, and in recesses in the ceiling. Not only will the light be thoroughly reflected, but there will be no visible sources to distract the eye.

This sort of ambient light is generally more pleasing than light from a single undiffused source, and it also harmonizes with the other two layers. While it is always essential to maintain the smaller spaces within rooms, you may also want to make some rooms seem larger. You can use light to soften the physical boundaries of rooms. Ambient lights placed high on walls to direct light up to the ceiling and lights concealed in cove moldings on ceilings create a sense of greater vertical space. Light can also be directed up or down whole walls—called *wall washing*—to make a room seem more spacious.

All these layers and practical considerations aside, though, ambient lighting does one other very important thing: it sets the stage for decorative light.

Above: Wall sconces direct light up to the ceiling to provide ambient light for this bathroom. Right: No central fixture can provide ambient light like this. Light from within the coves brightens the whole room without glaring or washing out the other lights.

Left: Ambient light provides a background for decorative light. Chandeliers come into their element when they can sparkle and not glare. Below: Candlelight filtered through glass votives and a tangle of Christmas lights make an intriguing combination of glowing light and shadow, turning an unused fireplace into the centerpiece of a room.

DECORATIVE LIGHTING

Decorative lighting is a layer freed from all obligation to do anything but shine and show off the beauty of light. It provides the element of sparkle and overt beauty in a lighting design and an outlet for your personality and creativity. It can also help emphasize important spaces in a room.

Decorative light can come from anything from a few candles or oil lamps to an elaborate crystal chandelier. It can mean a funky tangle of Christmas lights or a high-tech neon or fiber optic installation. From simple to high-tech, the essential element of decorative lighting is an interaction of material and light to create an object of beauty without-

out regard for utility—you're not lighting the room; you're making a statement.

Placing decorative light is a little like placing flowers or a sculpture: context is important. The light should be in a position to be admired. To provide a good context, other lights need to be adjusted. Being able to dim lights is a good idea in general, but it can be especially important for getting the maximum effect from decorative fixtures like chandeliers. If all the other lights in the room are off, the decorative light will

Decorative light can come from high- or low-tech sources. Right: Candlelight softened by paper lanterns balances the dark greens of the table settings and centerpiece. Below: Attention-gathering oversized paper lanterns work well in this light, simple decor.

become the only source of light—a bad thing because the contrast is too great, as when the chandelier glares against a totally dark background. If there are a few other indirect sources of light dimmed to a low level in the room, however, the contrast between light and dark will not be so great—and consequently your eyes will not have to make a radical adjustment. Everyone will be able to appreciate the chandelier without being blinded. In a large dining room, dimmable recessed lights near the chandelier can provide a perfect background.

The decorative light itself needs to be at the right level, too. Electric chandeliers should use bulbs of a fairly low wattage and luminescence. The goal is not to spread a lot of light around. In fact, for many decorative fixtures, the glowing filament of a clear low-wattage bulb creates much more sparkle than that of a high-output bulb, because you can actually look at it. Lightbulbs modeled on Edison's original bulb and other turn-of-the-century designs are available from specialty retailers. They not only add a period flavor to fixtures, but their low outputs can actually make decorative fixtures more striking.

Colors and Surfaces

Light fixtures aren't the only important factors in whether a room is well lit. All the surfaces in a room reflect light in different ways depending on their color and texture. Something as simple as a new coat of paint or a change in floor covering can make a huge difference in the way a room is illuminated. Even if you don't plan to make alterations, remember that light tends to accent textures and colors on walls and ceilings and position fixtures and choose bulbs accordingly.

Vibrant colors do make a room seem lighter and brighter. That's easy enough to see, but color and light can have a more complicated relationship. The color of a surface represents the colors of light being reflected back to your eyes—a red wall reflects mostly red light and absorbs more of other colors. That reflected light can sometimes bleed color onto adjacent surfaces. This can be quite pronounced in bathrooms, where surfaces tend to be shiny and brightly lit. One pink tiled wall or shower stall can make everything seem pink once the lights go on.

There are a few good lighting tricks to keep color from a bright, reflective surface from taking over. First, don't overlight the room. Avoid intense wall-washing lights on reflective walls, and stay away from bright, ambient sources near walls or ceilings. Focus instead on lighting task areas, and use large-sized frosted bulbs, which scatter light so that

Bright white light from these halogen lights picks up color from the highly polished surfaces in this hallway.

it arrives at a surface from a number of angles, making reflected color less pronounced.

Color isn't the only feature affected by light. Textures can be brought into the spotlight quite dramatically with well-placed light—just be sure it's the effect you want. Wall sconces and recessed lights can be positioned so they direct light down a wall at a slight angle, which accentuates any texture on the wall. Choosing a large-sized frosted bulb, which immediately diffuses light, cuts down on the severity of shadows and softens the appearance of textures. Small bulbs and bulbs with very focused beams do the opposite, casting hard, defined shadows by directing fairly focused light at largely parallel angles.

More pronounced, patterned textures, like relief in decorative plaster or a tin ceiling, are excellent candidates for their own dedicated accent lighting. Oblique accent light casts shadows that add depth and drama to shapes and textures. Even simple trim can be attractive in the right light. This is an ideal way to add ambient light while accenting a beautiful feature.

Highly reflective finishes on walls, floors, and countertops can also affect how a room is lit and especially how much ambient illumination it requires. Polished surfaces obviously reflect light more directly than matte or heavily textured finishes, and thus they can reduce the amount of artificial light needed to illuminate a space. Adding tile, stainless steel, or polished brass to a kitchen, for example, can significantly increase ambient light without adding a fixture.

The intense light from a halogen torchiere makes this rough brick wall appear even more imposing.

Color temperature and color rendering play a role in how light interacts with surfaces, as well. Incandescent light, with its warm, soft coloring, tends to blur shadows and complement darker colors and rougher finishes, while the clean, bright white light of halogen bulbs sparkles on more refined, polished surfaces.

Daylighting

Daylighting is a design and architectural concept much in fashion in new residential and commercial construction—and with good reason. Daylighting is the use of design and technology to increase the amount of daylight that enters a house and to control that daylight much the same way we control artificial lights.

A structure that incorporates daylighting has rows of windows near the ceiling, skylights, light tubes, and light shelves in conjunction with high-tech window glazing to get the most illumination out of the available natural light without heat or glare. The whole house can be positioned to account for regional variations in daylight, taking advantage, for instance, of the lower angle of winter sun, capturing precious natural light during short winter days while avoiding intensely hot direct summer sunlight. Cutting-edge designs even make use of mirrors to direct sunlight into spaces that would otherwise never receive any daylight.

All daylighting schemes try to increase natural light by creating places where light can pass into the house without causing glare or unwanted heat. By adding rows of windows above standard windows, architects and designers can introduce more direct sunlight into a room for more of the day. Adding a reflective shelf below the window helps spread the light across the ceiling, creating soft ambient light that brightens a room. These designs work particularly well in two story foyers and great rooms.

Small, high windows can also work well in small spaces. A well-placed window above a shower stall, for instance, can send natural light streaming into an otherwise dim enclosure.

Full-fledged daylighting designs generally are the work of expert lighting

High windows direct sunlight into rooms for ambient light without excess heat or glare.

designers and architects and realizing these designs can require extensive remodeling in existing homes. There are several less dramatic steps that you can take to introduce more natural light into a room.

Skylights and light tubes of all sorts can be added fairly easily to existing homes. Positioning the skylight so it will have maximum exposure to sunlight throughout the day can significantly brighten a room during the day.

Existing windows can be altered in any number of ways to increase the amount of light that comes through. Drastic changes, such as modifications to window framing, require the aid of an architect and a carpenter, but changes in drapes or shades or slight modifications to the window frame can also have an effect. South-facing windows where direct sunlight is intense are often so bright they have to be kept shaded. Adding an exterior overhang above the window can decrease direct light without cutting it off entirely or disrupting the view. A similar effect can be accomplished with landscaping—a trellis or well-placed climbing plant can diffuse intense sunlight.

Almost any room can be adapted to have more natural light. If you plan to make any major renovations or additions to your home, it's worthwhile to ask an architect about daylighting designs for your new or improved room.

Photo Courtesy of Lindal Cedar Homes Inc., Seattle, Washington

A crisp ray of sunlight is a welcome and refreshing addition to a morning shower.

CONTROLS AND FIXTURES

A huge variety of controls and fixtures are available to suit all needs and tastes. The following represents what is generally available.

Controls

Rocker switches are the direct descendants of the original toggle switch. They're easier for those with limited hand strength to use.

Rocker switch

Dimmer switches are the lighting designer's most important control. No lighting design can work if it can't be controlled to a finer degree than simply on and off. If you have easy control over the level of light, you'll be more likely to take time to set the lighting levels to suit the occasion. Dimmers also lengthen bulb life. Replacing a switch with a dimmer is a ten dollar–ten minute home improvement worth its weight in gold.

Dimmer switch

Motion sensing switches turn on lights as soon as you enter the room. They're perfect for bathrooms, hallways, and other rooms where fumbling for a light switch in the dark could be hazardous.

Integrated control panels are the home version of theatrical lighting control boards. By controlling several fixtures at once, you can create lighting schemes for specific times of day or situations using several fixtures dimmed to specific levels. Once you've created a scheme, all you have to do is press a button. Instead of switching on a light, these devices let you switch on the room.

Motion sensor

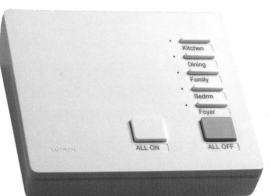

Photo Courtesy of Lutron

Integrated control panel

Fixtures

A. Chandeliers and pendants hang from the ceiling. Focused pendants provide light for tasks; fixtures mounted flush to the ceiling reflect light off the ceiling surface for ambient light; chandeliers provide decorative light.

B. Wall sconces are any fixtures that can be mounted on the wall. They provide ambient illumination by directing light up to the ceiling or down the wall.

C. Track lighting systems are flexible tracks installed on the ceiling that supply power to fixtures anywhere along the track. Fixtures include spotlights, pendants, and decorative fixtures.

D. Recessed lights are fixtures mounted inside a ceiling. They vary in size from one and one-half inches to eight inches and are available for interiors and exteriors, wet and dry locations. Depending on the trim (the part that directs the light), they can provide any light from very focused to diffused.

E. Strip lights are strips of small lightbulbs that can be installed under cabinets or shelves to create large task-lit spaces.

F. Torchieres are floor lamps that direct light up toward the ceiling to provide ambient illumination. They are generally placed near walls and in corners.

G. Cove lights are fluorescent tubes, flexible rope lights, or other small fixtures installed in coves, above cabinets, or behind trim to turn architectural features into light sources.

OUTDOOR LIGHTING DESIGN

Hail Twilight, sovereign of one peaceful hour!
–William Wordsworth

Pushing the darkness away from our homes and illuminating our yards at night is a timeless human pursuit. The porch light is an American icon as far back as the beginning of electric light. Victorians lit up their garden parties with paper luminaries, and torch light and bonfires have been a part of outdoor festivities since time immemorial.

There are many reasons for lighting the outdoors at night. Sometimes, we light the exteriors of our homes for very practical reasons—to make our homes safer or easier to identify. We also light spaces in our yards so that we can enjoy the evening without necessarily flooding it with light. We create outdoor extensions of our homes for night-time activities ranging from parties to private contemplation. We want to see and to savor the particular beauty of night.

Many of the principles of indoor lighting design are applicable to outdoor lighting—especially those concerning the definition of space. But outdoor lighting also presents its own unique design challenges and opportunities. When you bring light into a landscape, you are introducing two foreign elements: light fixtures and artificial light. If the fixtures, by their presence, disturb the nature of outdoor spaces, the design fails. If the presence of artificial light destroys the inherent beauty and mystery of the outdoors at night, not only does the design fail, it may become a nuisance to neighbors. Managing the balance of light and dark is paramount when lighting a landscape.

With care and planning, you can bring light into your landscape with beautiful and subtle effects. Well-planned lighting can improve safety and access and can carve spaces out of the darkness without destroying the majesty and mystery of night.

This chapter will guide you in adding fixtures to the exterior of your home, as well as using a variety of light sources from landscape lights to candles to create beauty and atmosphere in your landscape.

Safety & Security

Exterior lighting of homes and yards improves safety and security. It leads the way home by defining paths and entrances. It can illuminate an escape route in the event of danger or rebuff prowlers and other potential intruders. It can be a nuisance and an unnecessary expense, though, if it's not planned and controlled correctly.

Lighting walkways and entryways is a first priority. Path and entryway lighting guides you and visitors safely to your home. It marks steps and slopes and generally makes your home more accessible, but it also welcomes guests and should do so beautifully.

Dozens of fixture types are available for lighting pathways. Small downlights mounted on hook-shaped stakes provide focused illumination without wasting light. Lighted pavers can be built into brick walkways and lights can be recessed into decks and stairways. Traditional candlelit luminaries for special occasions or electrified versions for everyday are charming ways to light a path. Pathway lighting can also help define long or treacherous driveways for visitors.

Whatever fixtures you use, it is important to keep light on the path and not in your eyes. Against a backdrop of darkness, even a modestly bright light can be blinding if it points directly at eye level.

Entryways also need attention. Choose fixtures that can be mounted above eye level (at least 66") and that have covers to diffuse light and cut down on glare. Sconces on either side of a door provide ample illumination and nicely frame the door. If you use a single sconce, make sure it's on the keyhole side of the door.

Photo Courtesy of Intermatic Malibu Outdoor Lighting

A few low-voltage pathway lights can add style to a landscape while improving security.

Lighting around the perimeter of the house can provide a significant measure of security. Spotlights can be directed at the walls, especially near windows (don't aim light directly at windows), in dark corners, and around garages to discourage intruders. Conceal fixtures behind shrubs, or use units that can be buried. Recessed lights installed inconspicuously in soffits are perhaps the best choice for lighting the perimeter of a house. They are subtle and waste no light on the sky.

Controls are almost as important as fixtures and placement for effective safety and security lighting. As a rule, the more control, the better. Timers or photo cells can automatically turn on lights. For security lights, installing motion sensors at several points around the house allows specific areas or the whole exterior to be illuminated instantly whenever there is motion. For example, controlling driveway lights and lights above a garage door with a motion sensor triggered at the bottom of the driveway can make negotiating a dark and unfamiliar drive easier for visitors.

A well-lit entryway not only provides a measure of safety and security, but it makes a home more welcoming.

Photo Courtesy of Simpson Door Compnay

Lights on the pathway, the façade, and at the entryway make this house more welcoming and more secure.

Exterior motion sensors can also be configured to turn on interior lights in front rooms to brighten windows and make the house appear occupied. All motion sensors need to be placed and calibrated carefully so they're not continually crying wolf. Remote controls are another option and offer the greatest measure of flexibility. Units with key-chain-sized controllers can be installed to turn on or off almost any fixtures.

Having several control options also makes it possible for you to dim or turn off security and safety lights, allowing accent lights to do the work of creating an outdoor retreat for evening pursuits.

One last consideration—replacing lightbulbs in outdoor fixtures can be difficult. Perhaps the best improvement you can make to any standard-voltage outdoor fixture is to replace incandescent bulbs with compact fluorescent models (CFLs) rated for outdoor use. CFLs last nearly ten times as long—and they consume far less energy.

Light is a great tool for creating comfortable spaces in the outdoors. Right: Candles and a few small lights in the roof of the enclosure help create a comfortable garden sitting room. Below: Well-concealed lights accent the fountain and dramatically illuminate the hovering sculptures.

LIGHTING FOR BEAUTY

People spend thousands of dollars on decks and landscaping to extend their homes into the outdoors, but busy lifestyles mean that few of us are home during daylight hours to enjoy them. As a result, a huge outdoor lighting industry has sprung up to help homeowners enjoy their landscapes after the sun has set.

Outdoor lighting can do so much more than extend daylight hours. It can make the most of the unique atmosphere of your yard at night. Night transforms the outdoors, and it is a poor lighting design that fails to take advantage of the beauty of night and darkness. Lengthening shadows foster a sense of mystery and drama. Different plants and animals take center stage when the sun goes down. People have different moods and expectations for twilight hours. Outdoor lighting should be planned with all this in mind. With lights in place to ensure safety and security, a single layer of outdoor accent lighting can create whole living spaces where you can enjoy the unique nocturnal features of your outdoor home.

Candlelight is all the lighting needed for this romantic outdoor dining room. The flicker of dozens of candles complements the soft-edged beauty of the twilight landscape.

Outdoor accent lights must work against a background of near total darkness. Keeping bulb intensities low and light sources diffused is not only necessary for the practical purpose of preventing glare; it's also essential for preserving the atmosphere—you want to be able to see the stars and the fireflies, after all.

Gardens can be full of small, secretive spaces at night, and good lighting will gently accent them without revealing their secrets to the world. A vined arbor or a secluded garden niche is the epitome of romance and intrigue if a few soft, inconspicuous points of light graze its tangles and draw nighttime strollers into its confines.

In all spaces in your garden, let nature partially get in the way of light. Filter light through leaves and branches; the shadows will be welcome additions, and the fixtures themselves will be out of sight. Placing downlights overhead within the branches of a tree creates such a beautiful effect, and it doesn't waste light.

In flower beds, tiny uplights recessed in the ground or small spotlights can highlight specific plants. Sculptural objects like statues or fountains shouldn't be overlit. Light them softly from below or, with fountains, from within. Use colored lenses to soften and warm the light. As with indoor accent lights, in most cases a little illumination from the proper angle will capture attention better than bright light from all sides.

Decks are obvious places to add lights. Lights on steps and on the undersides of

Light sources recessed in the ground create striking effects. Right: A small buried spotlight throws dramatic light on this tree. Below: Lights on the perimeter of a deck provide a subtle glow and help define the edge of the deck.

railings provide very practical lighting for safety and accessibility, and outdoor cooking spaces can benefit from dedicated task lighting. The social spaces on your deck deserve soft, interesting sources of light. Gazebos and decks with arbors can be lit from above with pendants or even chandeliers. Japanese lanterns create soft, indirect light, while adding color and a sense of whimsy to the night. If there are no plants or flower boxes on your deck, consider adding some. Lights installed in and behind flower boxes and trellises accent plants and cast shadows that soften the rest of the space.

Electric lights aren't your only option for lighting social spaces outdoors. The lighting level requirements are low, so candles and torches provide perfect soft lighting that's well suited to the shadowy atmosphere. Candles also look spectacular against ice and snow in wintertime.

On smaller decks, a few candles in the center of a table will create a cozy gathering space. For large decks and patios, place clusters of candles where people congregate. Not only will the deck be softly illuminated, but it will sparkle from a distance.

Whatever spaces you choose to accent on your deck, patio, or in the garden, don't lose sight of the opportunities to create space and accent beautiful plants and objects. If you are creative and subtle, lighting will help you extend the spaces of your home beyond its walls.

Photo Courtesy of IKEA Home Furnishings

TASK & ACCENT LIGHTING IN PRACTICE

I f the preceding chapters have given you new insight into how light defines and shapes space, what follows will fuel your imagination as you create new lighting designs for your home.

Planning and installing new task and accent lighting based on the principles outlined in the Understanding and Designing chapters is easier than you might expect—and few home improvements can change the character of a room or a house so dramatically. The pages that follow contain dozens of photographs of designs in practice, with task and accent features highlighted. Use them as starting points for your own designs. Detailed instructions with how-to photos for installations come at the end of the chapter. Whether you do the work yourself or hire a professional, this chapter will provide you with ideas and guidance.

As with all home improvement projects, be sure to obtain the proper permits and schedule inspections before beginning. The basic wiring techniques chapter at the end of the book show wiring techniques for the projects, but if you are unsure of your skills, seek professional assistance.

Lamps are the workhorses of lighting design, providing flexible task lighting for any room.

A: Simple floor and table lamps brighten this bedroom, creating an inviting space to sit and providing comfortable, eye level reading light for

48

the bed. **B**: Well-placed lamps near seating areas help carve out spaces in large rooms.

Ceiling mounted lights such as pendant or track fixtures provide clutter-free lighting for all sorts of spaces. **C**: Pendants placed directly over task areas illuminate without getting in the way. **D**: The figure eight of low-voltage track lights puts light into all the spaces of this living room.

Adjustable floor lamps are perfect for creating small, intensely lit reading spaces. **E**: The "Tolomeo" lamp, designed by the famed Italian firm Artemide, is a modern classic.

Task lighting is crucial in the bathroom, where shadows can make you look tired and make grooming difficult. **F**: Simple wall sconces on either side of the mirror provide cross lighting for shadow-free grooming.

Photo Courtesy of Tech Lighting

D

See page 62 to install bathroom vanity lights.

Photo Courtesy of Room and Board

E

F

See page 64 to install under-cabinet lighting.

Kitchens are full of all kinds of spaces, each with unique lighting needs. **A**: Strip lights installed on the front edge of the undersides of cabinets are one of the best and easiest improvements you can make to lighting in a kitchen. **B**: Adjustable pendant lights, which can be raised and lowered as needed, provide bright and flexible task lighting for a kitchen counter. **C**: Strip lights provide continuous, intense task lighting for a work surface while recessed fixtures in the soffit above the breakfast bar shine gentler light for diners. **D**: Low-voltage track lights deliver very intense light to task spaces. This model is designed to replace a single central fixture. **E**: Softer task lighting makes eating spaces in this kitchen more inviting. **F**: Under-cabinet, recessed, and pendant lights all deliver light to task and social spaces in this kitchen.

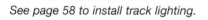

See page 58 to install track lighting.

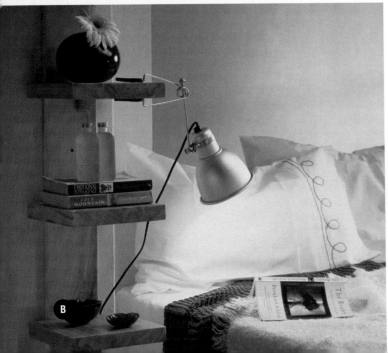

Beautiful task and accent lighting often comes from a few simple lamps. **A**: A table lamp does double duty, providing a welcoming space for reading and relaxing while accenting the orchid with light. The translucent shade provides a pleasant glow, while the height directs light at eye level—perfect for reading.

B: A simple clip-on utility light is a versatile, stylish, and very inexpensive way to create focused task or accent light. **C**: Lamps with opaque shades, like this floor lamp, reflect their light down, surrounding a space with light and casting a striking shadow on the wall.

Photo Courtesy of MIRAGE Prefinished Hardwood Floors

52

Built-in fixtures can also provide task lighting. **D**: Adjustable wall sconces replace traditional bedside lamps, preserving the clean, spare appearance of this room. **E**: Picture lights are a good way to show off paintings, but here an Arts and Crafts wall sconce adds a touch of style.

Good task lighting matches a room's decor and the other light sources. **F**: The warm light from the small table lamp harmonizes perfectly with the glow of the candles and the fire in the fireplace.

53

See page 60 to install low-voltage cable lights.

Built-in fixtures like track lights or recessed lights can bring accent light to cabinets and bookcases. Low-voltage recessed lights are tiny, bright, and produce very white, focused light. **A**: Recessed spots highlight the mantle and the grandfather clock in this living room. **B**: Installing low-voltage lights in a cabinet is easy and the effects it creates are sophisticated and beautiful.

Track lights mounted near walls also provide

See page 82 to install low-voltage recessed lights.

accent light for built-in cabinets and shelves.
C: Accent lights aren't just for art. Cable lights bring light to this pantry. **D**: These simple and easy-to-install surface-mounted lamps are cleverly designed to be placed on top of shelves to direct light down on the contents. **E**: For a sleeker look, these ceiling-mounted low-voltage spots provide sparkling light from inconspicuous fixtures. **F**: Pendant style fixtures can also be used creatively to light a display, as with this amusing take on the hanging bare bulb.

A

Accent lights in the right places can brighten a whole space. **A**: These well-placed recessed lights not only light up the cabinet and the painting, but brighten what otherwise might be a dim hallway.

Adding accent lighting is also an opportunity to set a mood for a room. Lights that just graze objects, cast shadows, or create warm pools of light all help accentuate a space's character. **B**: Candles bring their own unique powers to a painting and a few flowers. The motion of the flame keeps shadows swaying on the wall and draws the eye.

B

Accent light often means integrating indirect light sources into a display. **C**: A bare bulb and a couple of votives complete this display by providing glancing, dynamic accent light.

Fixtures that produce a less focused light can provide effective accent and ambient light. **D**: A not-so-simple floor lamp, complete with extra touches, throws a striking curve of light onto the paintings and illuminates the whole bedroom. **E**: A simple floor lamp brightens a corner and highlights this antique writing desk.

C

E

D

TRACK LIGHTING

Track lights give you the ability to aim ceiling- or wall-mounted light fixtures precisely for task and accent lighting. In a living room, for example, track lights can highlight artwork or favorite room accessories. In a kitchen, track lights can illuminate work areas and dining spaces.

Line-voltage and low-voltage track systems in all imaginable configurations and shapes are available for all these purposes and many others. Individual light fixtures from spotlights to pendants to decorative fixtures can be positioned anywhere along the tracks. A system might include intense spotlights for work areas and a soft, downlighting pendant for a dining area. The finished project is an effective and flexible lighting tool.

It's simple to replace an ordinary ceiling-mounted fixture with surface-mounted track lighting.

Tools and materials: *Basic wiring tools (see page 128), track lighting system, additional connectors and track, if necessary.*

1. To begin, turn off the power at the service panel, and test the circuit with a neon tester to make sure the power is off. Then, remove the old fixture if you are replacing an existing fixture.

If you aren't replacing an old fixture, install a new electrical box for the power supply and route cable to it from nearby receptacle (see page 131). Leave 11" of extra cable for making connections, and secure it in the box with a cable clamp. Remove 10½" of sheathing from the end, and strip ¾" of insulation from the ends of the wires.

2. Next, you'll install the power supply connector that feeds power from the circuit wires to the tracks. Connect the black circuit wire to the black power supply wire, and connect the white circuit wire to the white power supply wire. Connect the ground circuit wire to the power supply ground wire. Finally, attach the mounting plate to the electrical box with screws.

3. Mark the locations of all the tracks you plan to install. Tracks should be screwed into the framing in the ceiling or wall or anchored in the drywall with toggle bolts. Use a stud finder to find and mark the framing.

Mount the track that connects to the power supply first. Screw it into the ceiling, then secure the track to the power supply mounting plate with screws. Snap the power supply connector into the track and install the cover.

4. Install the other track sections, connecting them to the first track with connectors. Cap bare track ends with dead-end pieces. You can now restore the power and position the light fixtures to highlight work areas or to accent objects. If you're using a low-voltage system, make sure you don't add more fixtures than the wattage rating of the transformer allows.

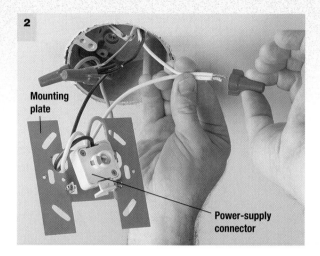

Mounting plate

Power-supply connector

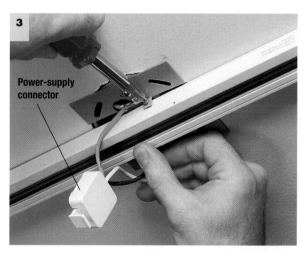

Power-supply connector

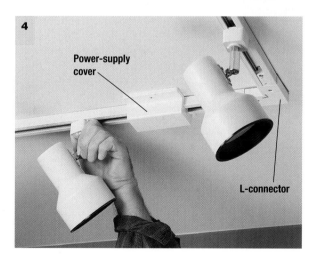

Power-supply cover

L-connector

LOW-VOLTAGE CABLE LIGHTING

This unique fixture system is a mainstay of retail and commercial lighting and is now becoming common in homes. Low-voltage cable systems use two parallel, current-carrying cables to suspend and provide electricity to fixtures mounted anywhere on the cables. The system's ease of installation, flexibility, and the wide variety of whimsical and striking individual lights available make it perfect for all kinds of spaces. Low-voltage cable light systems are ideal for situations where surface mounted track is undesirable or impossible to install. Most fixtures use the MR16 halogen bulb, which provides very white, focused light—excellent for accent lighting.

Tools and materials: *Basic wiring tools (see page 128), low-voltage cable lighting system.*

1. Screw the cable hooks into the walls, spacing the hooks 6 to 10" apart. (Make sure the hooks hit wall framing or use wall anchors.) Cut the cable to the length of the span plus about 12" extra for connecting the cable to the hooks and turnbuckles. Make loops at the ends of both cables with the provided fasteners, and attach the cables. Adjust the turnbuckles until the cables are taut.

2. Next, turn off the power at the service panel, and test the circuit with a neon tester to make sure the power is off. Remove the old fixture if you are replacing an existing fixture.

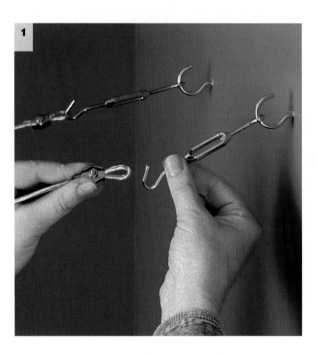

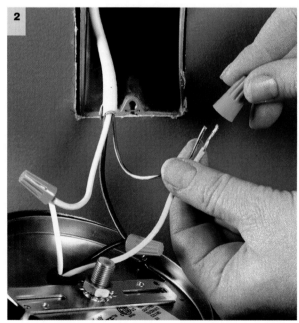

If you are not replacing an old fixture, install a new electrical box for the power supply and route cable to it from nearby receptacle (see page 131). Leave 11" of extra cable for making connections, and secure it in the box with a cable clamp. Remove 10½" of sheathing from the end, and strip ¾" of insulation from the ends of the wires.

Install the mounting strap for the transformer onto the fixture box with the provided screws. Remove the cover from the transformer, and connect the black transformer wire to the black circuit wire. Connect the white transformer wire to the white circuit wire, and connect the ground transformer wire to the grounding wire. Attach the transformer to the wall, and replace the cover.

3. Connect the two low-voltage leads from the transformer to the parallel cables. The low-voltage leads carry the 12-volt current from the transformer to the parallel cables that supply the fixtures and can be connected at any point on the cable and can be cut to any length. Connect the leads to the cables using the screw-down connectors provided. (It doesn't matter which lead is connected to which cable.) Make sure the screw is tight enough that it pierces the insulation. Once the leads are attached, it's safe to restore the power. The 12-volt current is safe, and it's easier to adjust the lights when they're on.

4. Attach the fixtures with the connectors

supplied by the manufacturers (fixtures connect in a variety of ways), and adjust the beams as necessary. Individual fixtures can be purchased at lighting stores, and you can generally mix and match manufacturers. Make sure you don't add more fixtures than the transformer can support.

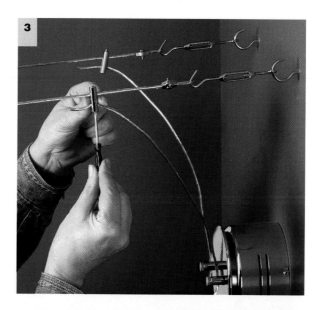

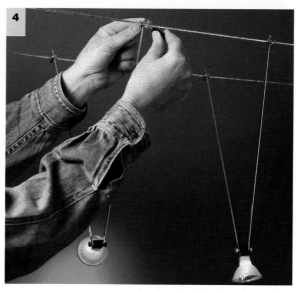

Vanity Lights

Many bathrooms have a single fixture positioned above the vanity, but a light source in this position misses the mark when it comes to providing good task lighting. Lighting from above casts shadows on the face and makes grooming more difficult. Adding sconces on the sides of a mirror is an easy way to get shadow-free cross lighting and keep the bulbs out of sight. The light sources should be at eye level; 66" is typical. The size of your mirror and its location on the wall may affect how far apart you can place the sconces, but 36 to 40" apart is a good guideline.

This project shows a very large strip of drywall removed for clarity; you may not have to remove as much. It is easier, though, to replace a large piece of drywall than to make several small patches (see page 136 for drywall information).

Tools and materials: *Basic wiring tools (see page 128), drywall repair tools, sconces and electrical boxes, nonmetallic cable, wire connectors, metal nail stops.*

1. Turn off the power at the service panel. Remove the old fixture from the wall, and use a neon circuit tester to make sure that the power is off. Undo the connectors, and remove the old fixture. Then, remove a strip of drywall from around the old fixture to the first studs beyond the approximate location of the new sconces. It's a good idea to make the opening large enough that you have ample room to route cable from the existing overhead fixture to the boxes for the sconces.

2. Mark the location for the sconces, and install new boxes. Install the boxes about 66" above the floor and 18 to 20" from the center-line of the mirror (the mounting base of some sconces is above or below the bulb, so adjust the height of the bracing accordingly). If the correct

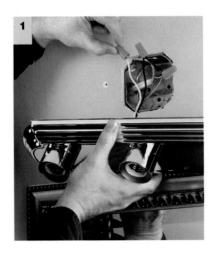

 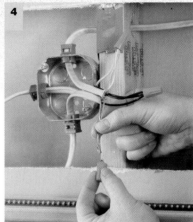

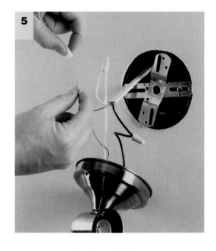

location is on or next to a stud, you can attach the box directly to the stud, otherwise you'll need to install bracing. Metal braces with adjustable electrical boxes (shown) are available at home centers.

3. Open the side knockouts on the electrical box above the vanity. Then, drill ⅝" holes in the centers of any studs between the old fixture and the new ones. Run two new NM cables from the new boxes for the sconces to the box above the vanity. Protect the cable from nails with metal nail stops, and secure the new branch cables at both ends with cable clamps, leaving 11" of extra cable for making the connection to the old box and new sconces. Remove 10½" of sheathing from the both ends of the cable, and strip ¾" of insulation from the ends of the wires.

4. Connect the white wires from the new cables to the white wire from the old cable with a connector, and connect the black wires from the new cables to the black wire from the old

cable. Connect the ground wires. Have an inspector check your work at this point. Then, replace the drywall, leaving openings for the sconces and the old box. You can cover the old box with a flat cover, or you can reconnect and reinstall the original above-mirror fixture after you've installed the new fixtures. You may want to replace the bulbs with low-wattage models.

5. Attach the fixtures by connecting the black circuit wire to the black fixture wire with a connector, and connecting the white circuit wire to the white fixture wire. Connect the ground wires. Finally, position the fixture over the box, and screw it down with the mounting screws.

UNDER-CABINET LIGHTING

Whether you are looking to add task lighting to a kitchen, office, or shop workspace, or you simply want to give a decorative accent to display shelving, under-cabinet lighting is a great choice. Under-cabinet lights come in several styles, including mini track lights, mini recessed cans (see page 66), flexible rope lights (see page 121), fluorescent task lights, and halogen or xenon strip systems (featured here). Strip systems are great for general task lighting on work surfaces, while individual recessed lights are best for highlighting selected spaces.

Some under-cabinet lighting systems plug into standard receptacles, while others are designed to be hard-wired into an existing circuit, as shown here. This installation shows hard-wiring a xenon strip under-cabinet fixture.

Ask an electrical inspector about code requirements regarding the type of cable required (some may require armored cable) and the power source from which you draw. Some codes may not allow you to draw power from a receptacle as shown in this project.

Tools and materials: *Basic wiring tools (see page 128), under-cabinet lighting system, dimmer, metal nail stops, nonmetallic cable, plastic switch box.*

1. Shut off the power to the receptacle you plan to draw power from, and use a neon circuit tester to confirm the power is off. Disconnect the receptacle from its wiring. Locate and mark the studs in the installation area, and mark and remove a strip of drywall for routing the cable.

Drill holes through the cabinet edging and wall surface directly beneath the cabinets where the cable will connect to the light fixture (inset). Drill ⅝" holes through the middle of the studs to run the cable, and protect the holes with metal nail stops. Install a plastic switch box. Route NM cable from the switch location to the power source, and route another cable from the switch to the first fixture hole. If

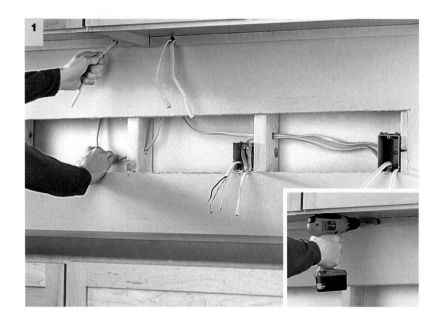

you are installing more than one set of lights, route cables from the first fixture location to the next, and so on.

2. Clamp the cable into the receptacle box with a cable clamp. Remove sheathing from the cable and insulation from the wires, and, using wire connectors, pigtail the white wires to the silver terminal on the receptacle and the black wires to the brass terminal. Pigtail the grounding wires together. Tuck the wiring into the electrical box and reattach the receptacle.

3. Remove the bulb, lens, and access cover from the light fixture. Open the knockouts for running cables into the fixture, and insert the cable into the knockout, leaving 11" extra for making connections. Secure it with a clamp. Attach the light fixture to the bottom of the cabinet with screws.

4. Remove 10½" of sheathing from the end of the cable, and strip ¾" of insulation from the wires. Use wire connectors to join the white circuit wire to the white fixture wire, the black circuit wire to the black fixture wire, and to join

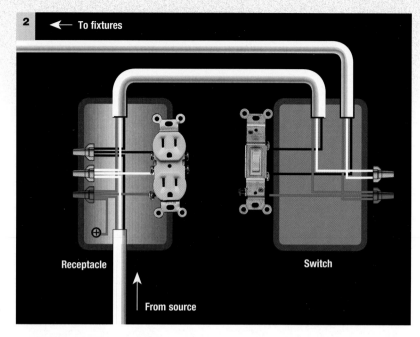

the ground wires. Some fixtures will require you to connect a second red wire along with the black and white wires (shown). Reassemble the fixture. Connect and install the switch by pigtailing the wires from the two cables to the switch terminals, and restore the power.

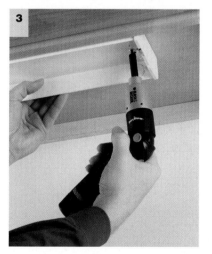

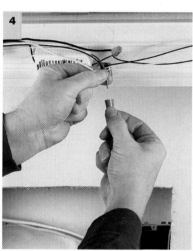

RECESSED LIGHTING

Recessed lights are versatile fixtures, suited for providing focused task and accent lighting or ambient lighting when installed in sets. Fixtures rated for outdoor use can also be installed in roof soffits and overhangs for accent and security lighting. Installing a single recessed fixture with a spot trim can provide task lighting for a work area or subtle accent lighting for artwork or an architectural feature.

Recessed fixtures can also be installed over showers or tubs. Be sure to use fixtures rated for bathroom use.

This project describes installing a single recessed light in a finished ceiling—if you can work from above, installation will be simpler.

There are recessed lighting cans in all shapes and sizes for almost every type of ceiling or cabinet. Picking the best one for your application will make installation much easier. Cans are rated as insulation compatible or for uninsulated ceilings. Be sure to use the correct one for your ceiling to prevent creating a fire hazard.

Tools and materials: *Basic wiring tools (see page 128), recessed can for remodeling and trim, nonmetallic cable, drywall saw.*

1. Turn off the power at the service panel. Make the hole for the can with a drywall saw or hole saw. Most fixtures will include a template

Recessed lighting fixtures

Recessed lighting trims

for sizing the hole. Use a fishtape to run the cable from the power source to a switch box and then to the hole (see page 132 for instructions on running cable and installing switches). Pull about 16" of cable out of the hole for making the connection.

2. Remove a knockout from the electrical box attached to the can, and thread about 14" of the cable into the box and secure it with a cable clamp. Remove 12" of the sheathing from the cable, and strip ¾" of insulation from the wires. Using wire connectors, connect the black fixture wire to the black circuit wire, the white fixture wire to the white circuit wire, and then connect the ground wire to the grounding screw or grounding wire (shown) attached to the box.

3. Install the can in the ceiling, depressing the mounting clips so the can will fit into the hole. Insert the can so that its edge is tight to the ceiling. Push the mounting clips back out so they grip the drywall and hold the fixture in place.

4. Install the trim by pressing the trim into the can until its spring clips snap into place. Restore the power and adjust the trim.

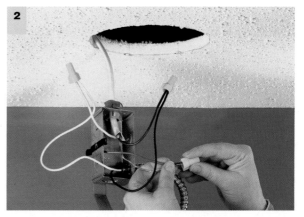

Ambient Lighting in Practice

Ambient lighting poses special challenges to lighting design. Improvements and additions to task and accent lighting will often change the amount of ambient lighting required in a room. You may choose to replace an old central fixture with track lighting or a decorative fixture, and a room that once relied on a single central fixture will suddenly have several sources for task and accent lighting. Additional ambient lighting can then come from less intense sources.

New, subtle sources of ambient light take imagination and creativity to plan, but once installed, they deliver beautiful effects. The photographs that follow illustrate the key principles of concealed sources and reflected light in context, as well as creative ways to gracefully integrate ambient lighting into a room. In the second half of the chapter, detailed instructions and how-to photographs guide you through installations of several basic ambient light sources.

A

Installing a number of concealed ambient light sources throughout a room has several advantages, not the least of which is the pleasant, diffuse light, completely free from glare. Concealed lights can also create visual effects on walls and ceilings. **A**: The very bright light fixture concealed above the niche creates a striking effect, allowing light to cascade in from above. **B**: Bold architectural features such as the slab-like soffits in this hallway stand out against a ceiling illuminated by lights placed on top of the soffits. **C**: Fluorescent tubes recessed in the coved ceiling of this kitchen provide plenty of general light for the kitchen without any glare.

B

C

A room needn't have elaborate architectural features to take advantage of concealed ambient light. **D**: Concealing rope lighting behind crown molding is another easy way to add a low level of ambient light to a room. **E**: Installing fluorescent tubes or strip lights above cabinets or shelves is a subtle—not to mention simple—way to brighten a room. **F**: Fluorescent tubes installed in recesses provide even light for this hallway, leaving the monolithic wall and ceiling surfaces uncluttered.

See page 84 to install crown molding lighting.

Photo Courtesy of IKEA Home Furnishings

See page 82 to install above-cabinet lighting.

Photo Courtesy of Lindal Cedar Homes Inc., Seattle, Washington

Surface-mounted fixtures can also provide indirect, reflected light suitable for bringing ambient light to all kinds of rooms. **A**: This wall sconce directs light up toward the ceiling, accenting the woodwork and illuminating the bathtub niche. **B**: These domed wall sconces mimic the shape of the circular windows. They also effectively brighten the wall around them with rings of light.

Sconces should always be placed where they won't direct light at eye level. **C**: Wall sconces with translucent bowls direct bright light up and softer light out into the room—perfect for lighting a hallway. **D**: Fixtures placed high on the walls give an impression of spaciousness. This

Photo Courtesy of Hubbarton Forge®

See page 78 to install wall sconces.

72

one illuminates the ceiling and gives a sense of the vastness of the room. **E**: Many manufacturers produce period-style wall sconces like this late 19th-century reproduction. The bottom fixture was originally intended for a bulb while the top would have held a jet for a gaslight—just in case. **F**: Sconces direct light up and down the walls of this grand entryway, emphasizing the room's scale. The sconces rise with the staircase, illuminating the path.

73

A

B

Ambient light sources can enhance the atmosphere of a room. Like good task and accent lighting, ambient sources help emphasize the details of a room. **A**: The simple torchiere in the corner of this room in Frank Lloyd Wright's "Fallingwater" house shines a plane of light across the ceiling, echoing the strong horizontal lines of the room.

Ambient lighting also serves important practical purposes in many rooms. For instance, indirect light is essential for entertainment rooms. **B**: Several flush-mount ceiling fixtures spread soft light around the room and set a perfect level of light for relaxing and watching television in this family room.

Entryway lighting should be bright enough to illuminate steps but soft enough to be welcoming. **C**: Wall sconces and accent lights fill this

74

stately entryway with warm light, while allowing the chandelier to sparkle.

Using fixtures that direct light up adds ambient light without glare. **D**: Pendants over this dining room table inconspicuously reflect their light up to the ceiling. **E**: Large windows darkened by twilight reflect light from this simple iron torchiere.

A

B

Beautiful ambient light can be the sum of all light from a variety of fixtures in the room. Controlling all the fixtures independently, preferably with dimmers, is essential. **A**: Shaded light fixtures, in the forms of table lamps, wall sconces, and a chandelier, work together to create a room with defined spaces and subtle ambient light. **B**: Nothing more than candles and sunlight from a window are necessary to light this room. The mirror over the mantle is a Victorian trick to increase natural light by reflection.

Several coordinated fixtures not only provide excellent light, but help to reinforce a room's style. **C**: A sleek, low-voltage track system powers several spotlights and two glowing pendants over the island. Fluorescent tubes concealed in the cabinet

C

tops round out this bright modern kitchen.

Many manufacturers specialize in reproducing antique fixtures for period homes. **D**: Reproduction fixtures harmonize with this Arts and Crafts-style room and provide inviting ambient light.

Useful ambient light isn't always artificial. Don't miss opportunities to use daylight for ambient light. **E**: Translucent window shades control glare as the sun sets.

WALL SCONCES

Wall sconces are great fixtures for supplying indirect ambient lighting in all sorts of situations. A couple of sconces can brighten up a dim hallway or replace a central fixture in an entertainment room for glare-free background lighting. Sconces can also frame an architectural fixture like a fireplace or large piece of furniture. Wall-mounted reading lamps with adjustable arms are also available—they're especially good alternatives to bedside table lamps. Sconces should be coupled with dimmers whenever possible for maximum control.

Some codes require switches at the top and bottom of staircases, so consult an electrician if you plan to install sconces along a staircase. This project shows two sconces installed with a switch at the end of the run, but the procedure is basically the same for a switch at the beginning of the run. You can install any number of sconces using the same steps.

Tools and materials: *Basic wiring tools (see page 128), two wall sconces and electrical boxes, nonmetallic cable, metal nail stops, dimmer switch.*

1. Mark the approximate locations of the new sconces and any new switches. Use a stud finder to locate and mark the studs around the area of the new sconces. Mark and remove an 8"-wide strip of drywall beginning at least 70" above the floor. The strip should begin in the center of the stud to the left of the far left sconce or new switch and end with the stud to the right of the far right sconce. Using the template included with the electrical box, make a hole for the switch in the drywall directly below the right sconce. Most codes require switches to be 48" from the floor.

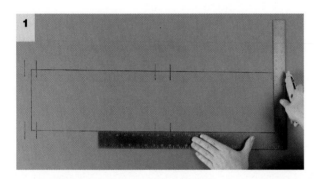

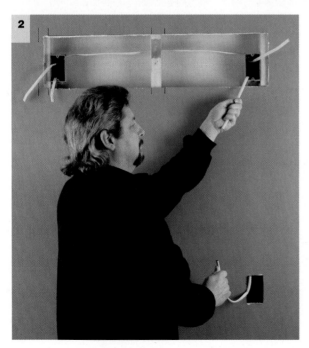

2. Open knockouts on the sides of the sconce boxes and on the top of the switch box. Install the boxes for the sconces. You can mount the sconce boxes directly to the studs or use bracing to support boxes between the studs. The light sources on the sconces should be above eye level—at least 72". Remember that the light source may be significantly above or below the base of the sconce; measure your sconce, and place the box so the light will be at least 72" above the floor.

Run a new NM cable from a power source to the nearest new sconce. Leave 11" of extra cable for making connections. Secure the cable with a cable clamp. Drill ⅝" holes in the center of each stud between the two sconces and between the second sconce and the switch box, if necessary. Install metal nail stops on the studs to protect the cable. Run another cable from the first sconce box through the holes in the studs to the next sconce box. Leave 11" extra on both ends. Secure the cable with cable clamps. Run another NM cable between the last sconce and the hole for switch. Leave 11" extra on both ends.

3. Remove the knock-out from the top of the switch box and pull the end of the

cable through. Secure it with a cable clamp. Place the box in the opening and secure it.

4. Remove 10½" of sheathing and ¾" of insulation from the wires on the ends of all the cables. If an inspection is required, have your work reviewed at this point. Replace and refinish the drywall (see page 136).

To wire the sconces, connect the black sconce wire to the two black circuit wires with a wire connector, and connect the white sconce wire to the two white circuit wires. Then, connect the grounding wire to the two ground circuit wires. Tuck the wires into the box, and attach the sconce to the box with the supplied mounting hardware. When both the sconces are wired and mounted on the wall, connect and mount the switch (see page 135).

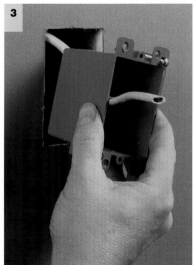
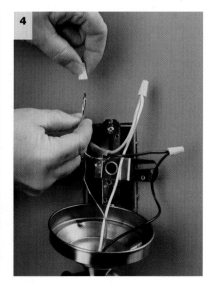

CUSTOM RECESSED LIGHT BOXES

Basements can be difficult to light adequately because the ceilings are too low for many light fixtures. Light boxes provide a perfect solution. High-quality fluorescent fixtures and tubes provide soft, flicker-free light, and the molding reflects and diffuses the light. The whole box fits between the joists, and can be sized to hold 2-, 4-, or 6-foot fluorescent light fixtures.

Whatever combination of molding and spacer pieces you use, it must project far enough from the box side to conceal the fixture from view but allow enough room for changing the tube. Spacers cut from 2× lumber combined with a 5 or 6" crown molding should work.

Tools and materials: Basic wiring tools (see page 128), carpentry tools, drywall repair tools, 2× lumber, crown molding, fluorescent fixtures, nonmetallic cable, reflective foil duct tape, light-colored semi-gloss latex paint, drywall.

1. Mark the box frame locations on the bottom edges of the joists. The inside of the frames should be about 2" longer than the light fixtures. Use a combination square to extend the layout lines onto the faces of the joists. Cut end blocks to fit, using the same size lumber as the joists. Set the blocks along the layout lines, and attach them with 3" wallboard screws (inset). Drill ⅜" holes through the end blocks and run

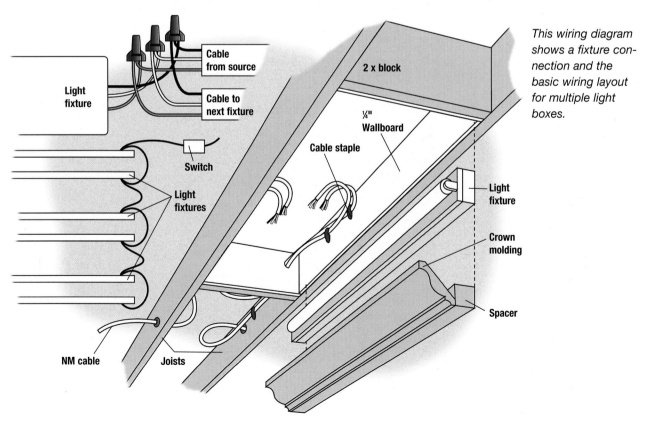

This wiring diagram shows a fixture connection and the basic wiring layout for multiple light boxes.

Light fixture

Cable from source

Cable to next fixture

Switch

Light fixtures

NM cable

Joists

2 x block

¼" Wallboard

Cable staple

Light fixture

Crown molding

Spacer

wiring for the boxes (see diagram at left). Cover all of the surfaces inside the box with ¼" dry-wall. Complete the drywall installation over the main ceiling surface, using ½ or ⅝" wallboard, then finish the outside corners of the box with corner bead. Tape and finish the inside corners of the boxes. Paint the entire surface inside each box with a light-colored, semi-gloss latex paint.

2. Install the fixtures in each box, positioning them so the lamp faces the center of the box. Center the fixtures from side to side, and fasten them to the joists with screws. Connect the fixture wiring to the circuit cables, following the manufacturer's instructions (see page 83).

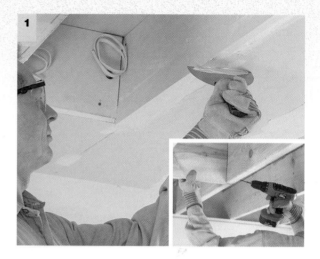

3. Cut the crown molding to fit snugly between the ends of the boxes. Paint the front faces of the molding, using the same paint used inside the boxes. Line the inside surfaces of each piece of molding with reflective foil duct tape. Determine the size of the spacers by positioning a piece of molding under a fixture with the bulb installed. Hold the molding away from the box side until you find the desired position. Then, measure between the molding and the box side to find the width of the spacer. Cut the spacer to width from 2× lumber (inset). Sand and paint the spacers to match the molding. Attach the spacers inside the boxes with wallboard screws. Make sure all spacers are level and at the same height. Attach the crown molding pieces to the front edges of the spacers with finish nails.

IN-CABINET AND ABOVE-CABINET LIGHTING

Cabinets are great places to hide all sorts of lighting. While under cabinet lights make great task lighting and accent lighting, cabinet tops and insides are great for concealing ambient sources. If you have space on top of wall-mounted cabinets, installing fluorescent tubes will provide ambient light by washing the ceiling—perfect for kitchens.

From within the cabinets, small recessed lights inside glass-door cabinets not only accent dishes and other collectibles, but can also provide indirect light for the whole room.

In-cabinet lights

Tools and materials: *Basic wiring tools (see page 128), mini low-voltage recessed light, 120 volt-12 volt transformer, hole saw.*

1. Use a hole saw to make a hole in the top of the cabinet or in a shelf. Depress the spring clips on the side of the light and fit it into the hole. The two wires should be on top.

2. Connect the light to transformer wires or to the next light in the series with wire connectors. The simplest way to install a transformer for these lights is to use a plug-in transformer. You can install a switch for the receptacle or you can use a plug-in transformer with a built-in switch. For larger, built-in cabinets, it may make sense to hardwire the transformer and use a standard switch or dimmer as with under- or above-cabinet lights.

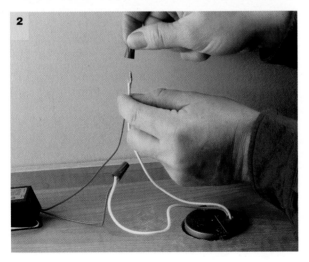

Above-cabinet lights

Tools and materials: *Basic wiring tools (see page 128), fluorescent light fixture, nonmetallic cable.*

1. Turn off power to the circuit and confirm that the power is off. Drill a ⅝" hole through the wall surface directly above the cabinets where the cable will enter each light fixture (inset). Route an NM cable from a nearby receptacle to a switch as you would for under-cabinet lighting (see page 65). Route cable from the switch to the hole above the cabinet. Use a fish tape to pull the cable up through the wall behind the cabinet. Pull about 16" of cable through the hole.

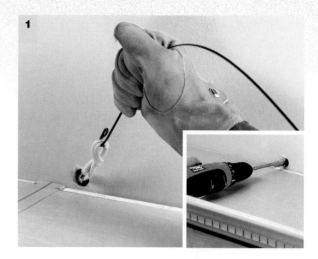

2. Use a fluorescent fixture that will be entirely concealed by the trim on the front edge of the cabinet top. (Lighting stores sell very low-profile fluorescent fixtures.) Remove the lens and the cover from the fluorescent fixture. Attach the light fixture to the back of the cabinet top with screws.

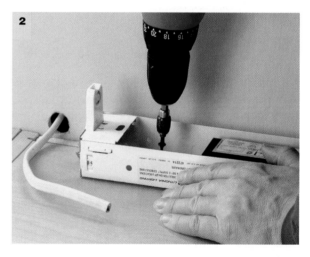

3. Remove a knockout from the fixture, and route the cable into the fixture, leaving 11" extra for making connections. Secure it with a cable clamp. Remove 10½" of sheathing from the cable and strip ¾" of insulation from each of the wires. Using wire connectors, connect the black circuit wire to the black fixture wire, and the white circuit wire to the white fixture wire, the grounding circuit wire to the fixture grounding wire. Tuck the wires into the fixture, and replace the cover and lens, and install a bulb. Install the switch, and restore the power.

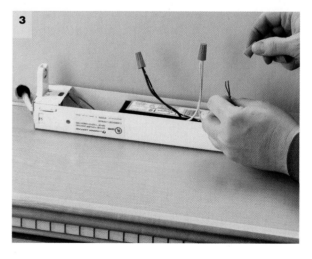

CROWN MOLDING LIGHTING

Rope lights hidden above a crown molding create soft, comforting light to wash walls and ceilings. The fixture works particularly well on light-colored walls. A stand-alone run along a wall can be used to draw attention to a room's focal point.

Rope lights can be easily adapted to any length of lighting run. Connect one rope to another by simply removing the end caps and inserting male/female connectors into the ends. This project shows line-voltage rope light being plugged into a receptacle. You can also hardwire low- or line-voltage rope light.

Tools and materials: *Carpentry tools, crown molding, 2× lumber for blocking, 6d finish nails,*

3" screws, rope lighting. (See Resources, page 138)

1. Use a stud finder to locate studs in the installation area. Mark the stud locations with light pencil marks near the ceiling, making sure the lines will be visible when the trim is in place. Plan the layout order of the molding pieces to minimize cuts and avoid noticeable joints. Also keep in mind the location of the receptacle that you plan to plug the rope lighting into. To maximize light reflection from the walls and ceiling, position the molding 3 to 12" from the ceiling. Measure from the ceiling and mark points at the ends of the wall to represent the bottom edge of the molding, and then snap a chalk line between the marks.

2. Because the crown molding will not be fastened at the top, it is necessary to install support blocking. Use a bevel gauge to determine the precise angle of your crown molding. Rip 2 × 2 lumber to this angle, using a table saw or circular saw. Fasten the supports to wall studs using 3" screws. The supports can be installed in long strips or cut into 6" blocks and attached at each molding joint and every 4 feet

1

3" to 12"

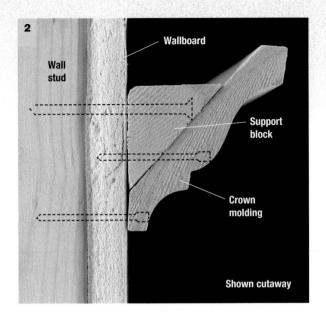

2

Wall stud

Wallboard

Support block

Crown molding

Shown cutaway

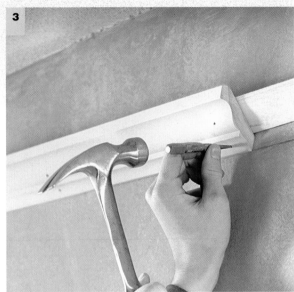

3

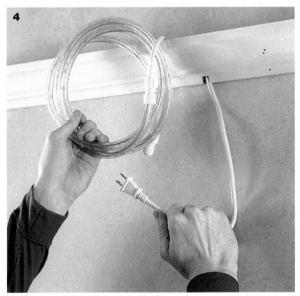

4

on long runs of molding.

3. Set the molding in place along the chalk line. Have a helper hold the molding in place as you drill pilot holes and fasten it with 6d finish nails. Drive one nail into the stud along the lower edge of the molding and one into the support blocking. Use a nail set to recess the nail heads slightly.

4. Install the remaining sections of molding. When you are above the receptacle you will use to power the rope lighting, cut a small notch in the molding with a jig saw and lay the cord in the notch before fastening the molding to the wall. Follow the manufacturer's instructions to join or cut any segments of rope lighting to the proper length. Lay the rope light in the trough between the wall and molding and work it around the entire installation. Plug in the light to activate it.

Variation: Flip the molding upside down and attach it to the wall for a down-lighting cornice effect. Attach the rope lighting in the cornice with mounting clips, sold separately.

DECORATIVE LIGHTING IN PRACTICE

L ight possesses a certain unique beauty that people have always recognized and sought. From Christmas lights, to birthday candles, to neon signs, light plays a role in all sorts of situations, and it can be a pleasing part of any decor. Start to see light and light fixtures as objects of beauty and materials for creativity, and you'll open a new avenue for expression.

Whether your taste inclines toward homemade lamps or antique chandeliers or contemporary lighted sculpture, this chapter will whet your appetite for decorating with light. You'll find dozens of eye-catching fixtures and valuable advice on how to place any decorative light for maximum effect. The Resources section (see page 138) contains a listing of retailers and designers who specialize in decorative light fixtures.

You don't need to buy manufactured light fixtures, though. Some of the most satisfying decorative lights will be the ones you create yourself. The second half of the chapter features several projects and ideas, complete with detailed photographs and instructions, to get you started on creating your own decorative fixtures.

A

Lighting translucent sculpture from within creates a subtle form of decorative lighting that can become the focal point of a room. **A**: Simple incandescent bulbs light up the eye-catching artisan-paper sculpture from within, accenting the texture of the paper and creating shadows. **B**: Lighting from within highlights the shape and color of this Akari lamp by 1950s designer Isamu Noguchi.

Chandeliers and hanging lighted sculpture

B

C

make beautiful and attention-gathering decorative fixtures in any space. **C**: Dozens of shining glass facets make this star fixture stand out against the color of this wall. **D**: Low-wattage clear bulbs give an effect similar to candlelight. Control them with a dimmer so they are just slightly brighter than the background light.

Don't just hang fixtures in the center of a room. Hanging fixtures tend to become focal points, so place them where they will help emphasize the spaces within rooms. **E**: The hanging cubes shift the emphasis in the room to the corner, where they cast soft shadows. **F**: The rustic candelabra provides a sparkling, glare-free decoration for a table in this cabin-style dining room.

See page 94 to install a hanging light fixture.

See page 96 to make a candle chandelier.

89

See page 98 for creative uses of low-voltage lighting.

Photo Courtesy of Tech Lighting

Photo Courtesy of Hubbardton Forge®

An element of whimsy and ecclecticism is a welcome addition to decorative lighting. **A**: A menagerie of lighted figures descends from the ceiling in a child's bedroom from this low-voltage track system. A huge variety of fixtures are available for these systems. **B**: Thrift-store and found objects combine with photographic transparencies to make an intriguing display. **C**: Sometimes the combination of simple, clean materials—wrought iron and a translucent light-ed cylinder, in this case—make the most attrac-tive statements.

See page 92 to make a lamp.

Never underestimate the humble table lamp when it comes to interesting decorative light. **D:** There is no three-dimensional object yet invented that can't be turned into a lamp of some sort. **E:** Any old lamp can get a new lease on life with the right lamp shade. Plain lamp shades can be covered with almost any fabric or paper for a wide range of results.

Christmas lights are good for a lot more than trees. **F:** Strings of lights are woven with vines and sheer fabric to create a beautiful garland for any season.

MAKIN LAMPS

Making lamps is easy. The basic procedure is always the same. Thread the lamp cord through the base and up to the socket, and then connect two wires. With imagination and a few parts available at hardware and craft stores, you can make anything into a table or floor lamp.

1. Thread the lamp cord through the base and up through the lamp pipe and socket cap. Split the end of the cord so you have two wires about 3" long. Strip about ½ to ¾" of insulation from the ends of the wires. Tie an underwriter's knot (inset) by forming an overhand loop with one wire and an underhand loop with the remaining wire; insert each wire end through the loop of the other wire.

2. Loosen the terminal screws on the socket. Look carefully at the insulation on the wires—the insulation on the "hot" wire will be rounded and on the neutral wire it will be ribbed or will have a fine line on it. Loop the hot wire around the socket's brass screw and tighten the screw. Loop the neutral wire around the socket's silver screw and tighten the screw. Adjust the underwriter's knot to fit within the base of the socket cap, then position the socket into the socket cap (inset). Slide the insulating sleeve and outer shell over the socket so the terminal screws are fully covered and any slots are correctly aligned. Test the lamp; when you're sure it works, press the socket assembly down into the socket cap until the socket locks into place.

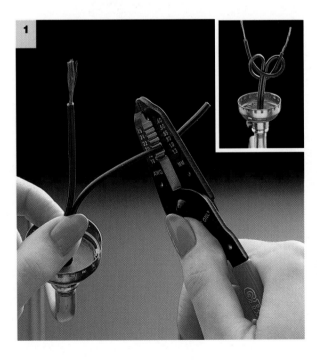

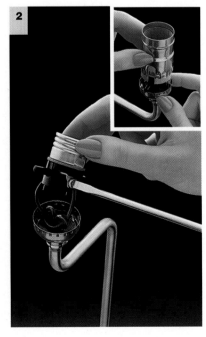

TEACUP LAMP

Tools and materials: *Basic wiring tools (see page 128), lamp cord, threaded rod, 1" brass couplers, lamp base, bulb socket, lamp shade harp, teacups and saucers.*

1. Drill a ½" hole in the center of each cup and saucer. Stack the teacups and measure them. Purchase a threaded nipple from a hardware or lamp store that will accommodate the stack and leave about ½" at the top; purchase one 1" coupler for each inch of the nipple. Slide a lock washer and a hex nut onto one end of the threaded nipple. Insert the nipple into the hole of the lamp base. Place a rubber washer over the nipple.

2. Set the first cup and saucer in place, add a rubber washer and a brass washer, then screw four brass couplers onto the threaded nipple. Add a brass washer and a rubber washer, the second cup, and a second set of washers; repeat to add the third cup. Screw on four more

couplers, and top the assembly with a threaded brass washer, a lamp shade harp, and another threaded brass washer.

3. Attach a socket cap to the nipple. Insert a lamp cord through the base and the nipple. Tie the split ends of the wire in an underwriter's knot, connect them to the lamp socket, and assemble the socket. Add a lampshade and, if desired, a finial.

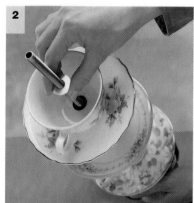

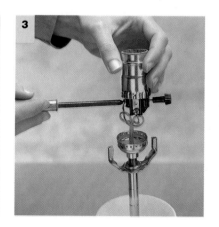

CHANDELIERS AND PENDANTS

Ceiling mounted globe fixtures are good targets for replacement in any room. In most cases, they provide poor ambient light or a lot of glare. Consider using other sources for ambient lighting

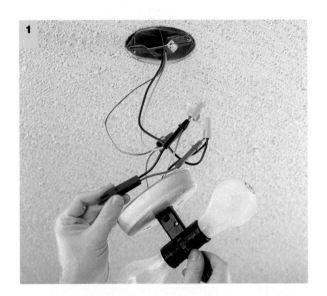

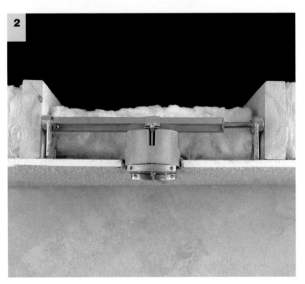

and replacing the ceiling fixture with a chandelier for decorative sparkle or a pendant for task lighting. Another good option is a fixture that mounts close to the ceiling but washes the ceiling with light instead of directing light down. The wiring is easy, so maneuvering a heavy crystal chandelier on top of a ladder may be the most challenging part of the project.

A decorative chandelier should be low enough so the light catches eyes but not so low that it blinds them.

Tools and materials: *basic wiring tools (see page 128), hanging fixture, specified bracing.*

1. Shut off the power at the service panel. Remove any ornaments or shades, and the bulbs. Detach the old fixture by unscrewing it at its base. Without touching the bare wires, use a neon circuit tester to make sure the power is off. When you're sure the power is off, disconnect the old fixture base by unscrewing the wire connectors.

2. If the new fixture is much heavier than the original fixture, it may require additional bracing in the ceiling to support the electrical box and the fixture. As a general rule, fixtures under 25 pounds will work on standard boxes and bracing. Beyond 25 pounds and with all ceiling fans, additional bracing is necessary. The

manufacturer's instructions should specify. If the ceiling is finished and there is no access from above, you can remove the old box and use an adjustable remodeling brace appropriate for your fixture (shown). These are available at home centers and lighting stores. Once the bracing is in, install a new electrical box specified for the new fixture.

3. Adjust the length of the fixture's hanging support before wiring or attaching the base. Most chandeliers have chains with removable links. Some pendant fixtures use a plastic tube to make the pendant hang straight down. Test the fixture's height before making the chain length permanent. Cut the power cord a foot longer than the chain so you will have enough wire to make connections.

4. Attach the cross brace to the electrical box with screws. Thread the fixture mounting ring

onto the threaded tube in the center of the cross brace. Close the top link of the hanging chain around the mounting ring.

5. Weave the cord from the fixture through the chain and push it through the threaded tube and into the box. Pull a few inches of the cord down. Separate the two wires and strip ¼" of insulation from the ends. Connect the white circuit wire to the neutral cord wire. (The neutral cord wire will have ridges along its length or a colored stripe.) Connect the black circuit wire to the hot cord wire. Attach the ground circuit wire to the grounding screw on the box.

CONVERTED CHANDELIER

This book repeatedly sings the praises of candlelight as an ideal form of light. There's no reason why this ideal shouldn't be a reality in your home—or at least be an option for special occasions.

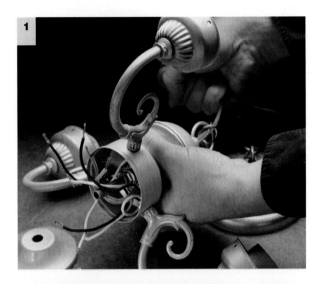

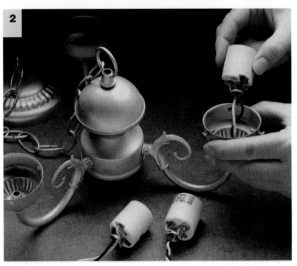

Chandeliers are perfect showcases for candlelight because they were meant to be objects of beauty rather than the sources of general light into which they've evolved. With dimmable indirect light sources providing a low level of ambient lighting, the warm, sparkling, glare-free light of candles draws all eyes to the chandelier without being blinding.

Any electric chandelier, whether an antique store find or one from a garage sale, can be modified for candles without much trouble or cost. A lamp store should have the parts needed for this project and for other additions. The Resources section (see page 138) of this book can direct you to any parts or materials you can't find in your area. For finishing your creation, a wide variety of easy-to-apply finishes and antique patinas are available.

Make sure the candles are well below the ceiling, and never leave lit candles unattended.

Tools and materials: *needlenose pliers, chandelier, candleholders, bobeches, flat lamp bolts.*

1. Remove any glass globes or lightbulbs from the chandelier. Remove the cover at the bottom of the center part of the chandelier. It should be held on by a decorative cap that unscrews. Disconnect all the wires, and pull the cord out from the top of the chandelier.

2. Unscrew the bulb sockets. Most chandeliers have bulb sockets that are screwed onto a short threaded rod attached to the arm. Turn the socket counter-clockwise until it is free of the rod. Pull out the sockets and wires connected to them. If your chandelier has a collar that held globes, you may have to unscrew and remove it before you can attach the candleholders.

3. Install a chandelier candleholder on each arm by placing it over the threaded rod. You may also wish to install a bobeche (as pictured). A bobeche is a decorative metal or crystal collar that fits under the candleholder and catches wax dripping from the candle. Secure the holder with a washer and a thin lamp nut.

Instead of chandelier candleholders, you could also use small wooden candle cups, teacups, or demitasse cups drilled out to accept the threaded rod; just be careful not to unbalance the chandelier. Select a holder appropriate for the candle size you want to use—not all chandeliers need use tapers.

4. Apply a finish, if desired. (If you intend to use crystal bobeches or teacups as candleholders, apply the finish to the chandelier before installing.) First, apply a coat of metal primer, and allow to dry. Finish with paint or antique finish (as pictured). Replace the chain and install.

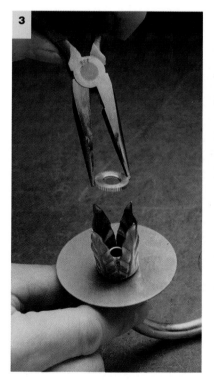

LOW VOLTAGE/
HIGH STYLE

The best lighting designers win renown not only for their ability to use light to accent and improve architectural spaces, but for their creative, cutting-edge fixture designs and installations. Unfortunately, expense and the dangers of 120-volt household current make doing anything with light fixtures beyond making lamps a rather daunting proposition for many people.

Low-voltage lighting offers another option. Low-voltage cable lighting systems are often-used and flexible tools for contemporary lighting designers, but their relatively low price and wide availability also make them perfect vehicles for your own creativity.

The systems are simple. A transformer lowers household current to a safe 12 volts and then feeds it to two parallel cables. Fixtures draw power when they are clipped to the cables. Since the voltage is so low, little or no insulation is needed and code restrictions are few. Most home centers carry low-voltage cable kits with plug-in transformers and three or five halogen fixtures. The kits cost around $50 and are meant to be quick-and-easy track lights (see page 60), but they can also be the raw material for your own designs.

Part of the beauty of low-voltage lighting is its safety and ease of use, but some care should be exercised. You can't harmfully shock yourself with the 12-volt current, but you can short circuit the

transformer and possibly damage it. Also, halogen bulbs get very hot when in use, so never allow flammable materials to come in contact with them. Finally, modifying a kit will almost certainly void any warranty it might have.

With a little care and creativity, you can make unique designs with these simple, inexpensive products. Here are just a few ideas:

Making fixtures

"Chopsticks," the rigid metal rods included in many cable lighting kits, carry current from the cables to the bulbs, but any conductor will do in their place. In the images on this page, coated and uncoated aluminum wire replaces the chopsticks. The aluminum wire can be shaped to form curves or twists, among other things. The clamps included with the kit hold the wire to the cable, and a ring terminal connects each wire to the bulb holder.

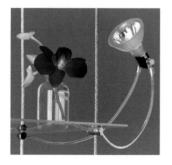

Making or modifying low-voltage fixtures this way is easy, but the principles of electrical conductivity still apply. If you use uninsulated materials to make fixtures, the two sides must not touch or they will short circuit the system. Beyond this, the possibilities for what you can create are almost endless, and all the materials are available at good hardware stores or home centers for a few dollars.

Wired deskset

Cable lights can work in a variety of decors, but their clean, simple lines and industrial look work especially well with simple metal and light-colored wood pieces. This project turns an inexpensive mass-produced piece of furniture into something unique.

Using cable lights to add functional and eye-catching lighting to the department-store deskset below required little more than drilling a few holes for hardware and guiding the cables through the shelves.

Eyescrews on the bottom of the top shelf turn the cables across the desk and back down the other side. The mounting hardware included with the cable lighting kit connects the ends of the cables to the bottom shelf.

You can tailor the light to the workspace by replacing the bright, high-wattage bulbs included in the kit with less intense, lower-wattage bulbs. A 25-watt bulb can provide very good task lighting on the work surface while 10- to 15-watt bulbs softly accent objects on the shelves.

You can also add other features not shown here. A length of low-voltage rope light (see page 121) or low-voltage mini recessed lights (see page 82) can be tied into the cables.

When you're done, you've turned a simple desk into a unique piece of furniture.

Floating shelves

This set of shelves seems to float on thin cables. It required only a lighting kit, three squares of clear 8" × 10" plastic, eyescrews, bare 10-gauge aluminum wire, and ³⁄₃₂" uncoated steel cable—all available for less than twenty dollars at a home improvement center. The result is a graceful combination of lighting and display space.

The shelves won't hold much weight, but they're perfect for small, three-dimensional pieces that cast interesting shadows.

The two cables run from the eyescrews anchored in the floor through holes drilled in the corners of the plastic squares. Eyescrews anchored in the ceiling turn the cables across the ceiling and then back down through the other side. The connectors included in the kit hold the shelves in place (see inset) and make the electrical connections for the fixtures.

Clear plastic is widely available in precut 8" × 10" sheets, which work great as shelves, but you could use any lightweight material in its place. Larger shelves could be used with additional cables for support. Lighting stores that sell cable lights should be able to supply additional connectors (see the Resources section on page 138 for additional suppliers). You can use the fixtures included in the kit or fabricate your own, as shown.

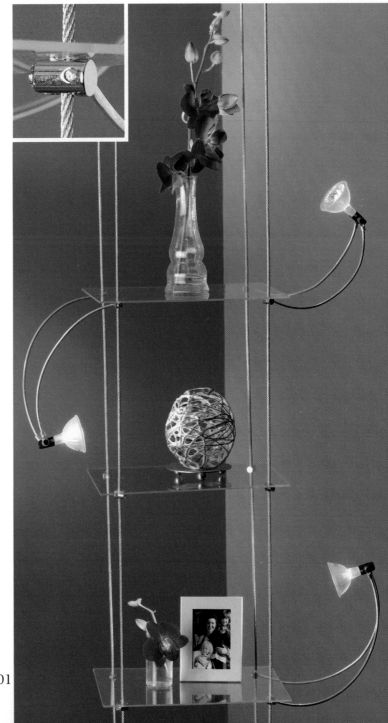

Outdoor Lighting in Practice

Adding outdoor lighting is one of the most eye-catching improvements you can make to the exterior of your home. And it's also one of the simplest to do yourself.

There are as many opportunities to create spaces and accent details outside your home as there are inside. You can extend your home's livable area by making comfortable, serene spaces on decks and patios and in gardens, and light can be a powerful tool for doing this. Adding lighting to landscaping and to the exterior of a house improves security and accessibility, and, when done well, it creates a distinct nighttime personality for your home.

Every home and landscape is different and deserves a unique lighting design. Seek out unique fixtures and plan a design that provides just the right mood for the setting.

The photographs in this chapter contain dozens of ideas for imaginative outdoor lighting, but they're only the beginning. Use them to fuel your own imagination as you work on a design for your outdoor home. When it comes time to install fixtures, the second half of this chapter will show you several basic projects, complete with photos, to get you started.

Photo Courtesy of Lindal Cedar Homes Inc., Seattle, Washington

When the sun goes down, a few well-placed lights on the exterior walls help to extend rooms into the outdoors by softening the contrast between indoors and out. **A**: Several wall sconces help balance the light on this patio with the indoor lighting, making it a pleasant place to relax after the sun sets. **B**: Lighted pavers, stake lights, and small spotlights highlight the pathway and accent landscaping features as they brighten this front yard.

For areas where light fixtures will be visible, take the time to look beyond the widely available

Photo Courtesy of Kerr Lighting

low-voltage fixtures. The Resources section (see page 138) of this book provides contact information for several manufacturers and retailers. **C**: A simple hanging lantern fits the peaceful mood of this shaded garden.

Dozens of manufacturers produce beautiful low- and line-voltage outdoor fixtures. **D**: Reproduction period pieces, like these classic gas light-style lanterns, add a touch of style to exterior lighting.

Most outdoor spaces don't have ceilings or walls for mounting ambient fixtures. Recessed floor lights are a good option when you need to provide a lot of light without cluttering the space with fixtures. **A**: Watertight recessed lights provide ample illumination for this pool deck without taking up space.

In gardens, concealed light sources often make the boldest statements. **B**: Spotlights recessed in the ground behind this garden cast light up through the plants, creating imposing shadows while illuminating the fountain and the sculpture.

A

B

Lighting your home's façade not only improves accessibility and security, but it enhances its appearance by accenting and highlighting its best features. **C**: Lights placed behind the shrubs inconspicuously accent the stonework on this home. **D**: Lights concealed in the ground in front of this house frame the window as they illuminate the façade. Path lights mark the walkway. **E**: Soffit-mounted downlights accent landscaping as they light the front of this house.

Photo Courtesy of Intermatic Malibu Outdoor Lighting

Photo Courtesy of Lindal Cedar Homes Inc., Seattle, Washington

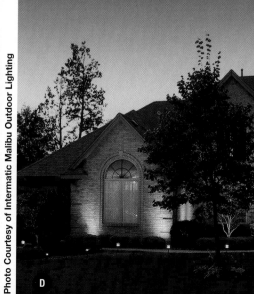

Photo Courtesy of Intermatic Malibu Outdoor Lighting

Placing lights in ponds and fountains creates beautiful effects. **A**: Submersible spotlights shimmer in this tile-lined pond. **B**: Tiny spotlights concealed beneath translucent glass create an enchanting glow in this garden fountain.

Low-voltage path lights are available for a variety of landscape styles. **C**: Bulbs embedded in these pavers light up the path through the snow. **D**: Flower-shaped lights are inconspicuous among the landscaping. **E**: Canopied stake lanterns are easy to install, creating pools of light for a pathway without flooding the darkness.

See page 122 to build a lighted tile fountain.

A

B

There's something about candlelight and lengthening shadows that invites people to slow down and relax—just the thing for a patio or a deck. Candles, torches, and lanterns are perhaps a little more trouble than electric lights, but the atmosphere they create is worth a few minutes and a couple matches. **A**: Candle-lit hanging lanterns add festive flair to any occasion. **B**: Tall and slender wrought iron candleholders provide beautiful and flexible light for this elegant patio.

Candlelight comes to life when set against water. **C**: The reflective surface of this garden pool multiplies the light from the candles.

Candlelight is unmatched when it comes to carving out a private space for a quiet dinner,

C

relaxing with a book, or just communing with the fireflies. **D**: An antique candelabra lends its light to this sheltered corner of a garden.

E: Candles add their special elegance to this table for two.

Make using candles an outdoor habit. Leave inexpensive votives in glass holders around patios and decks. If they're always there, you're more likely to use them. Be creative with candleholders. **F**: In the winter, ice block luminaries are an elegant and easy way to get a striking effect with candles. They require little more than freezing a full bucket of water.

D

F

E

FLOODLIGHT

Floodlights provide safety illumination for outdoor spaces like driveways and garages. They can also be an important part of any security system. When controlled by a motion sensor, they can illuminate large areas around the house instantly and help discourage intruders.

The steps that follow show how to install a new floodlight and switch in a garage. You can also install one on the exterior of the house and install a switch inside.

Tools and materials: *Basic wiring tools (see page 128), carpentry tools, plastic electrical boxes, nonmetallic cable, cable staples, floodlight, switch.*

1. Turn off the power to the circuit that operates the receptacle to which you'll be wiring the floodlight. Position the light fixture box against the inside sheathing of the garage wall, adjacent to a stud. Outline the box on the sheathing, then cut a hole with a reciprocating saw. Position the box so its edges extend into the cutout, then attach it to the adjacent stud.

2. Attach the switch box to the side of a stud inside the garage, located near a GFCI receptacle. Cut one length of NM cable to run from the light fixture box to the switch box, with 1 foot extra at each end. Anchor the cable to the garage framing every 4 feet to within 8" of the boxes, using cable staples. Cut another length of cable to run from the switch box to the receptacle box, allowing 1 foot extra at each end. Anchor it with cable staples. Remove 11" of sheathing from both ends of each new cable, and strip away ¾" of insulation from the ends of the wires.

3. Open a knockout in the light fixture box. Insert the new cable into the box through the knockout opening, so that about ½" of the cable sheathing extends into the box, and secure the cable with a cable clamp. Assemble the light fixture

according to manufacturer's instructions. Attach the black fixture wire to the black circuit wire. Attach the white fixture wire to the white circuit wire. Connect the fixture grounding wire to the circuit grounding wire. Carefully tuck the wires into the box, and attach the light fixture faceplate to the fixture box.

4. Open a knockout in the top and bottom of the switch box. Insert the new cables from the fixture and from the receptacle into the box through the knockouts, so about ½" of the cable sheathing extends into the box. Secure the cables with cable clamps. Install the switch (see page 135).

5. Use a neon circuit tester to make sure the GFCI receptacle power is off. Remove the cover, gently pull the receptacle from the box and detach the wires. Open a knockout in the box,

using a screwdriver, and insert the new cable, so that about ½" of the cable sheathing extends into the receptacle box. Secure the cable with a cable clamp. Join the grounding pigtail on the GFCI to the circuit grounding wire and the grounding wire from the switch using a wire connector. Attach the white circuit wire (the one from the power source) to the silver GFCI screw terminal marked LINE. Attach the black circuit wire to the brass screw terminal marked LINE. Attach the white wire running from the receptacle to the switch to the silver GFCI screw terminal marked LOAD. Attach the black wire leading to the switch to the brass screw terminal marked LOAD. Tuck all wires back inside the box and carefully press the receptacle into the box and secure it with mounting screws. Install the cover and restore the power.

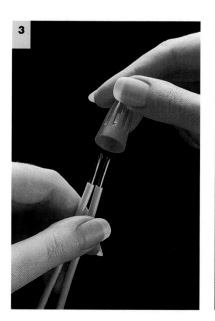

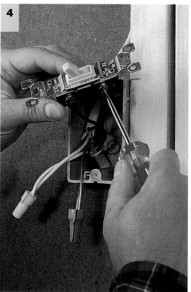

LOW-VOLTAGE LANDSCAPE LIGHTING

Low-voltage outdoor lighting systems are the easiest way to bring accent lighting to a landscape. The basic system is simple: A transformer connected to an outdoor receptacle steps household voltage down to a safe 12 volts. Cable then carries current to individual fixtures. Installation is easy, and you don't need a permit or an inspection. Home improvement centers carry a

variety of fixtures, transformers, and controls, as well as all-in-one kits.

Kits are a quick and easy way to add a few lights, but if you take the time to make a plan for your landscape and to pick your own fixtures, you can create a unique and customized landscape lighting design.

Planning

First determine what you want to light. You'll need to know this to purchase fixtures and the right transformers. Make a sketch of your yard, including locations of receptacles. Take a look around your yard at night, and identify the things you want to light. Mark locations for lights, including decks, arbors, patios, and other features. Light pathways every 8 to 10 feet.

Once you've decided what you want to light, you can pick fixtures. Fixtures are available to light almost anything, so stretch your imagination. Consult catalogs and Internet retailers in addition to home improvement centers to get a better idea of what's out there. All 12-volt fixtures will work together so you can mix and match manufacturers.

After you've decided on fixtures, note the wattage of all the lights you plan to use and add them to your diagram. Once you've filled in the wattages, you can begin mapping out circuits. The illustration on page 115 shows several

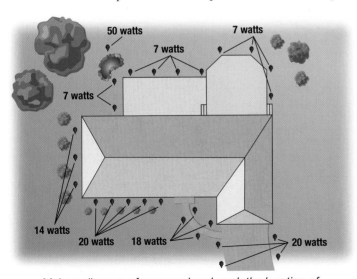

Make a diagram of your yard and mark the location of new fixtures. Note the wattages of the fixtures and use the diagram to plan circuits.

common circuits. Draw cable paths onto your diagram, keeping in mind obstructions like sidewalks or driveways. Lengthy cable runs or too many fixtures on a single cable can result in dim lights, so plan multiple circuits and avoid long cable runs (see the chart below).

Some designs may work better if you use several smaller circuits and transformers instead of one high-wattage transformer and one large circuit. For example, if you want to light a back deck as well as front landscaping, install separate systems for greater control and ease of wiring.

Once you've mapped out the circuits and determined how many separate systems you want to use, add up the wattages on each system. Purchase transformers with enough capacity to handle the loads plus at least 25 watts. If you plan to use submersible lights, be sure to purchase a transformer rated for them.

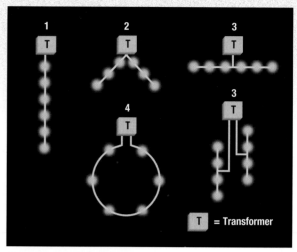

Common circuit layouts
1. **Serial circuits** work best for simple designs with short cable runs.
2. **Split circuits** allow you to run two cables the maximum distance from the transformer.
3. **Tee circuits** distribute power evenly to lights that must be placed far from the transformer. You can also split the load over two tee circuits. Cable splices should be soldered and insulated with electrical tape.
4. For more compact designs, **loop circuits** provide the most even power distribution.

Circuit length	Cable Gauge	Max Watts
up to 100'	16	150 w
100-150'	14	200 w
150-200'	12	300 w

Recommended cable lengths and gauges.

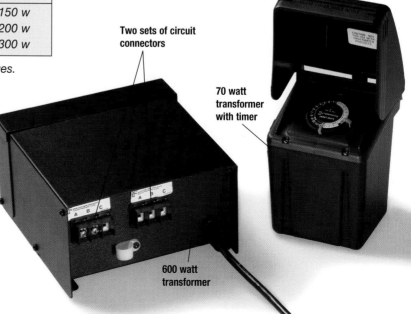

Two sets of circuit connectors

70 watt transformer with timer

Outdoor transformers are available in wattages from 60 to 1000. If you have two circuits, purchase a transformer with two sets of hook-ups.

600 watt transformer

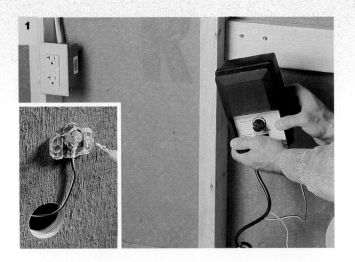

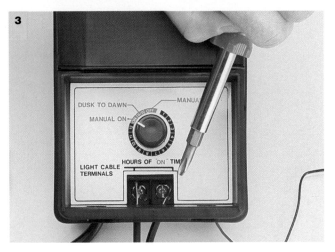

INSTALLING LOW-VOLTAGE LANDSCAPE LIGHTING

Tools and materials: *Basic wiring tools (see page 128), drill, outdoor transformer, outdoor cable, fixtures, cable connectors.*

1. Install your transformer or transformers. If you are installing one in a garage or shed, mount it on a wall within 24" of the GFCI receptacle and at least 12" off the floor. Drill a hole through the wall or rim joist for the cable and any sensors to pass through (inset). If you are using an outdoor receptacle on an exterior wall or a post (see page 124), mount the transformer on the same post or an adjacent post at least 12" off the ground and not more than 24" inches from the receptacle. Do not use an extension cord. Many codes require that outdoor receptacles have watertight covers.

2. If a circuit begins in a high-traffic area, it's a good idea to protect the cable by running it through a short piece of PVC pipe or conduit and then into the shallow trench.

3. Connect the cable to the transformer. Use the appropriate gauge cable for your circuit load (see page 115). Strip just enough insulation from the ends of the cable to make a good connection with the screw terminals. Make sure

there is 10 feet of cable between the transformer and the first fixture in the circuit. If you are running cable from a transformer on a post, staple the cable to the post an inch or two from the ground.

4. Lay the cables for each circuit. For routing around and under decks, use cable staples to hold the cable in place. Place the fixtures and connect their wires to the circuit cable. If drain pipes or irrigation systems are nearby, you may want to adjust the pipe or the fixture to minimize moisture contact.

If you are making tee circuits, most manufacturers recommend soldering the cable splices.

5. Connect all the fixtures to the circuit cables. The fixture wires run from the fixture to the circuit cable and connect with special connectors which pierce the insulation on the cable and the wires to make a watertight connection.

Most fixtures either rest in the ground or on a stake, but for fixtures mounted in trees, be sure any fasteners you use are stainless steel or cadmium-plated steel. Other materials may poison the tree.

6. Check to make sure the lights are working before you conceal the cable. You can use a voltage tester to make sure you are getting 10 to 12 volts at the point where you want to install your fixture. (Losing two volts to voltage drop on any one circuit is considered acceptable.)

CONTROLS AND ACCESSORIES

Many outdoor transformers come with a built-in timer and several *trippers*—movable pins for setting on and off times—but a number of other devices are available to provide greater control.

Photo sensors can be added to most transformers to turn on the lights when the sun sets for dusk to dawn operation.

Motion sensors can be added to any system to help deter intruders. Choose a model with a timer to control the sensor's active period. Be sure to place the sensing unit where it won't be inadvertently activated by normal traffic.

By adding a remote control unit to a transformer, you can turn on pathway and other lights as soon as you pull into the driveway.

Manufacturers also offer a variety of replacement bulbs in various wattages so you can fine-tune the light coming from a single fixture. Colored bulbs and filters are also available for adding color to lighting designs, a particularly effective strategy in submersible lights.

A variety of devices for controlling and automating outdoor lighting: (A) photo sensor, (B) remote wireless motion sensor and timer, (C) wireless remote control and receiver.

Techniques & Tips

Cable running along walkways is more likely to be disturbed by foot traffic. To protect the cable at sidewalk and path edges, dig a shallow trench with a spade and press the cable into the trench.

Conduit, metal tubing that protects electrical wires, can help in running cable under cement sidewalks. Cut a length of 1" metal conduit about 1 foot longer than the width of the sidewalk, then flatten one end with a hammer to form a sharp tip. Dig short trenches a few inches deeper than the depth of the cement on either side of the walk. Drive the conduit through the ground under the sidewalk with a hammer, using a block of wood to protect the end. When the sharp tip comes through the other side, cut it off so the cable can pass though. Run the cable through the conduit and fill in the trenches.

When very long cable runs are unavoidable, use a multi-tap transformer. These transformers can compensate for long cable runs by raising the voltage at the beginning of the run by a few volts.

Fountains are a welcome addition to a garden. Any 12-volt fountain pump, available at garden stores and through specialty fountain retailers, can connect to a low-voltage outdoor lighting system.

Use a spade to dig a shallow trench to protect cable runs in high-traffic areas.

For cable runs that cross a sidewalk, drive metal conduit under the concrete and feed the cable through.

RECESSED STEP LIGHTS

Low-voltage recessed lights are great for decks. Installed inconspicuously in the deck boards, they provide accent lighting for plant boxes or pathway lighting for stairs.

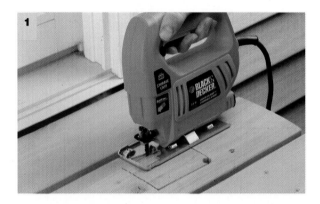

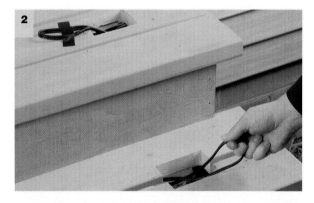

Tools and materials: *Basic wiring tools (see page 128), jig saw, recessed deck lighting kit, outdoor low-voltage cable.*

1. Use the template or trace the bottom of the fixture onto the treads to mark holes for each light. Center the fixture on the tread, 1 to 2" from the edge (the hole will center on the gap between the 2 × 6s on most deck stairs). Cut the holes with a jig saw. Test the fixtures to be sure they will fit (they should fit snugly), and adjust the holes as necessary.

2. Run cable from an existing low-voltage system or from a new transformer to the stairs. Drill a hole in the bottom riser if necessary, and snake the cable under the stairs along the inside edge. Pull a loop of cable through each of the holes for the fixtures and temporarily secure it to the tread with tape.

3. At the middle of the first loop of cable in the series, separate 3 to 4" of the two conductors in the cable by slicing down the center. Strip about 2" of insulation off of each wire. Cut the wire in the center of the stripped section, and twist the two ends and the end of one of the fixture wires into an outdoor wire connector. Secure the connection with electrical tape. Repeat with the other fixture wire and the other circuit wire. Tuck the wires back into the hole, and place the fixture into the hole. Test each fixture before installing the next one.

DECK RAILING LIGHTS

Rope light is thin, flexible clear tubing with tiny light bulbs embedded every few inches along its length. Most rope lights are meant to plug into a receptacle and use household current. While this is all right for indoor decorating, it limits their use outdoors. Low-voltage versions, however, are powered by transformers and can be connected inconspicuously to a low-voltage landscape lighting circuit. They are available from specialty lighting stores and catalogs.

Tools and materials: *Basic wiring tools (see page 128), rope lighting, U channel, low-voltage outdoor cable and connectors, cable staples.*

1. Run a cable from a transformer or from a nearby low-voltage circuit using a T connector.

Route the cable up a post at the end of the rail, and secure it with cable staples. Leave enough length at the end of the cable to connect it to the rope light.

2. Secure the rope light to the underside of the railing with U channel. Cut the channel to length, and nail it to the bottom of the railing. Press the rope into the channel.

3. Connect the fixture cord to the end of the rope with the twist-on fitting. Connect the rope wires to the branch cable with a cable connector designed for low-voltage outdoor cable. Cap the end of the rope with a plastic cap.

CERAMIC TILE FOUNTAIN

A fountain in a garden pond looks great in any landscape. Add lights and a splash of color with ceramic tile and you've got a striking water feature. Building and installing one is much easier than you'd imagine.

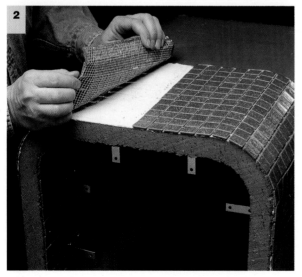

Twelve-volt fountain pumps can be wired into any low-voltage lighting system. This fountain uses tiny submersible disc lights to provide illumination, but a wide variety of submersible lights are available. The chimney flue used for the base of the fountain can be purchased at fireplace and masonry stores.

Tools and materials: *Basic wiring tools (see page 128), 12-volt fountain pump, submersible 12-volt lights, ceramic tile, thinset mortar, grout, 8 L brackets, ¾" expanded metal grate, landscape fabric, bricks, construction adhesive, 18 × 18" chimney flue, 2 to 3 pounds of sea glass.*

1. On the inside of the flue, draw a line about 6" from the top. On each wall of the flue, position two L-brackets with construction adhesive. Smear adhesive on one side of each bracket and press it into place so the horizontal part of the bracket is flush with the line and the bracket points down. Remove each bracket immediately and allow the adhesive to cure for 10 minutes. Reset the brackets.

2. Plan an arrangement for the ceramic tile. Set the tile with thinset mortar on the outside, top, and inside the flue down to the 6" line. After letting the mastic dry according to the

manufacturers instructions, grout the tile.

3. Position four bricks at the bottom of the water garden and set the flue on them. (The flue is very heavy so recruit a helper or two for this.) Set a concrete block in the center of the flue, put the lights and fountain pump on top of it, and run its leads out the bottom of the flue. Cut the expanded metal grate to fit inside the flue. In the center of the grate, use bolt cutters to expand a hole to approximately 1" in diameter. Place the expanded metal grate on the L brackets. Run the tube from the fountain pump through the center hole, positioning it so it is just slightly higher than the edge of the flue. Place the lights on top of the grate and run the wires out the bottom of the flue. Run the wires

from the pump and the lights to the nearest low-voltage cable in your landscape lighting system. Connect the pump and fixture wires to the cable with connectors. If you don't have a low-voltage lighting system in place, run the cables to a transformer and plug in the transformer at the nearest GFCI outlet. Test the pump and adjust the operation of the pump as necessary. Dig a small, shallow trench and bury the cables.

4. At the center of the grate, stack sea glass to resemble a volcano, with the fountain discharge tube at the center. Use silicone to stick the individual pieces together, offsetting the joints as much as possible. Cover the remaining grate with a layer of loose sea glass.

GARDEN POST GFCI RECEPTACLE

If exterior receptacles are in short supply or they're just too far from the landscaping you'd like to light, adding a garden post GFCI may be the solution. Receptacles can be installed almost anywhere in a yard to power lighting or provide electricity for power tools.

The following sequence illustrates a basic method for creating a freestanding receptacle anchored to a wood post embedded in a bucket of concrete. The receptacle is wired with UF (underground feeder) cable running through a trench from a junction box inside your house or garage. Sections of conduit protect the outdoor cable where it's exposed.

If you'd like to attach the outlet to an existing landscape structure, such as a deck, fence, or gazebo, you can modify the project by attaching the receptacle box and conduit to that structure. Keep in mind that freestanding receptacles should be at least 12", but no more than 18", above ground level.

Before you begin this project, have your local inspector review your plans and issue a work permit. If local code requires that your work be inspected, schedule these visits at the appropriate points during the project.

Tools and materials: *Basic wiring tools (see page 128), LB connector, metal sweeps, 1" metal conduit, compression fittings, plastic bushings, pipe straps,* *2-gallon bucket, 4-foot post, outdoor receptacle box, 12-gauge UF cable, GFCI receptacle.*

1. Plan a convenient route from an accessible indoor junction to the location you've chosen for the receptacle. Drill a 1"-diameter hole through the exterior wall, near the junction box. Mark the underground cable run from the hole in the wall to the location for the receptacle. Carefully remove 8" to 12" of sod along the marked route, then dig a trench that's at least 12" deep.

2. Install the LB connector on the outside of the hole. Measure and cut a length of conduit about 4" shorter than the distance from the LB

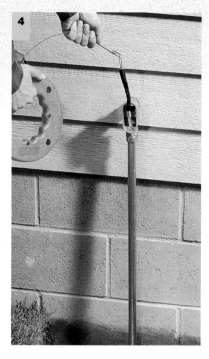

connector to the bottom of the trench. Attach the conduit to a sweep fitting, using a compression fitting. Attach a plastic bushing to the open end of the sweep to keep the sweep's metal edges from damaging the cable. Attach the conduit assembly to the bottom of the LB connector, then anchor the conduit to the wall, using pipe straps. Cut a short length of conduit to extend from the LB connector through the wall to the inside of the house. Attach the conduit to the LB connector from the inside of the house, then attach a plastic bushing to the open end of the conduit.

3. Drill or cut a 1½" hole through the side of a 2-gallon plastic bucket, near the bottom. Mount the receptacle box to the post with galvanized screws. Position the post in the bucket. Measure and cut a length of conduit to run from the receptacle box to a point 4" above the base of the bucket. Attach the conduit to the receptacle box and mount it to the post with pipe straps. Insert a conduit sweep through the hole in the bucket and attach it to the end of the conduit, using a compression fitting. Thread a plastic bushing onto the open end of the sweep. Dig a hole at the end of the trench. Place the bucket with the post into the hole, then fill the bucket with concrete and let it dry completely.

4. Measure the distance from the junction box in the house out to the receptacle box. Cut a length of UF cable 2 feet longer than this measurement. At each end of the cable, use a utility

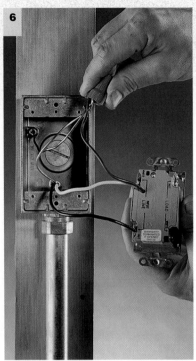

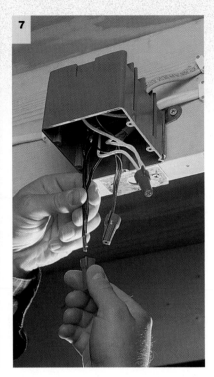

knife to pare away 8" of the outer sheathing. Lay the cable along the bottom of the trench from the house to the receptacle location. Open the cover on the LB connector and feed a fish tape down through the conduit and out of the sweep. Feed the wires at the end of the UF cable through the loop in the fish tape, then wrap electrical tape around the wires up to the sheathing. Using the fish tape, carefully pull the end of the cable up through the conduit to the LB connector.

5. At the other end of the trench, feed the fish tape down through the conduit and out of the sweep. Attach the exposed wires to the loop in the fish tape, and secure them with electrical tape. Pull the cable through the conduit up into the receptacle box. About ½" of cable sheathing should extend into the box. Connect the cable with a cable clamp.

6. Using wire strippers, remove ¾" of the wire insulation around the two insulated wires extending into the receptacle box. Attach a bare copper pigtail to the grounding terminal on the back of the receptacle box. Join the two bare copper wires to the green grounding lead attached to the GFCI, using a wire connector. Connect the black circuit wire to the brass screw terminal marked LINE on the GFCI. Connect the white wire to the silver terminal marked LINE. Carefully tuck all the wires into the receptacle box, then mount the receptacle. Install the cover plate.

7. From inside the house, extend the fish tape through the conduit and LB connector. Attach the cable wires to the fish tape, then pull the cable into the house. Anchor the cable along framing members to the junction box, using cable staples. Turn off the power to the junction box, and remove the junction box cover. Test the circuit with a neon tester. Use a screwdriver to open a knockout in the side of the junction box, and then pull the end of the UF cable into the box through the knockout, and secure it with a cable clamp. About ½" of the outer sheathing should extend into the box, and the individual wires should be about 8" long. Using a wire stripper, remove ¾" of the wire insulation from the insulated wires. Unscrew the wire connector attached to the bare copper grounding wires inside the box. Position the new grounding wire alongside the existing wires and replace the wire connector. Using the same technique, connect the new black wire to the existing black wires, and connect the new white wire to the existing white wires. Replace the junction box cover and restore the power to the circuit. Fill the trench and replace the sod.

VARIATION: WIRING INTO AN EXISTING RECEPTACLE

Instead of wiring your garden GFCI receptacle into a junction box, you can wire it into an existing receptacle in your basement or garage. Before you begin, turn off the power to the existing receptacle.

1. Remove the cover plate and the receptacle. Test the circuit with a neon tester.

2. Open a knockout in the side of the receptacle box with a screwdriver. Pull the end of the UF cable into the box through the knockout and secure it with a cable clamp.

3. Detach the circuit wires connected to the receptacle. Connect a bare copper pigtail to the ground screw terminal on the receptacle, a white pigtail to a silver screw terminal and a black pigtail to a brass screw terminal.

4. Using a wire connector for each set of wires, join the bare copper grounding wires, then the white neutral wires, then the black hot wires.

5. Carefully tuck the wires and receptacle back into the box. Replace the cover plate and restore the power.

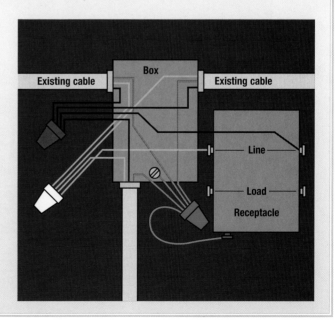

Basic Techniques

Basic Tools

Most fixture installations require the wiring tools pictured below, as well as basic carpentry tools. Having the proper tools will make any light fixture installation quicker and easier, not to mention safer.

The basic techniques and tips that follow will help you through many of the situations you will encounter when installing new fixtures, but this book does not cover every wiring scenario.

A comprehensive wiring guide like *The Black and Decker Complete Guide to Wiring* is a valuable resource for additional information. Consult a professional electrician if you are unsure about how to proceed with any project.

For new installations where you will be adding new cable or tying into a receptacle, most local codes will require you to apply for a permit and have an inspector look over your work before you connect the fixtures.

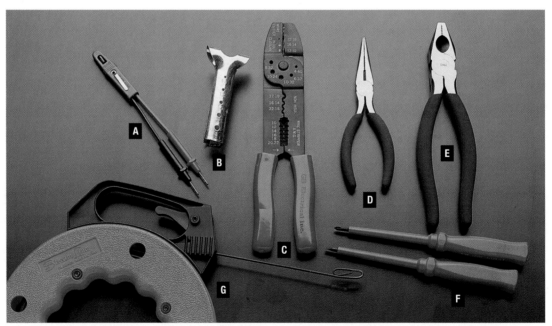

A) A neon circuit tester is used to test circuit wires for power. B) Cable rippers remove the outer sheathing from NM cable. C) A combination tool can cut cable and cut and strip wire. D) Needlenose pliers bend and shape wires for making connections to switch and receptacle terminals. E) Lineman's pliers are useful for cutting and pulling cable and for twisting wire together. F) Insulated screwdrivers reduce the risk of shock. G) Fishtape helps snake cable through finished walls and ceilings.

Basic Wiring Skills

Using a neon circuit tester

Use a neon circuit tester to make sure that the power is off to the circuit you're working on.

After shutting off power to the circuit, detach the receptacle or fixture by removing the cover plate and the mounting screws. Carefully pull the receptacle or fixture away from the box, taking care not to touch the bare wires. Touch the tester probes to the hot and neutral terminals. The tester will not glow if the power is off. If the tester glows, switch off the proper circuit breaker before doing any work.

Removing wire insulation

Strip ¾" of the insulation from each wire in the cable, using the wire stripper openings on a combination tool. Choose the opening that matches the gauge of the wire, then clamp the wire in the tool. Pull the wire firmly to remove the insulation. Take care not to nick or scratch the ends of the wires.

Connecting two or more wires

Hold the wires parallel, then screw a wire connector onto the wires. Tug gently on each wire to make sure it's secure. The wire connector cap should completely cover the bare wires.

Always make sure you use connectors sized for the wire gauge you're using.

Using a neon circuit tester

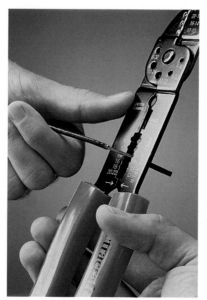
Removing insulation from wires

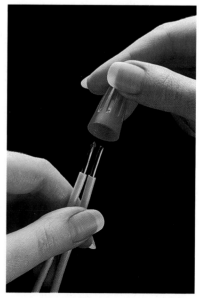
Connecting wires

CABLE

If you add new fixtures in new locations, you will have to run new electrical cable from a receptacle or other power source. All the projects in this book assume you're working with 15 amp circuits, for which you will need *14/2 nonmetallic (NM) cable,* plastic cable containing two insulated 14-gauge wires (hot and neutral) and a bare ground.

The steps on pages 132-133 will help you run cable through existing walls and ceilings without disturbing much drywall. If you're not comfortable running cable, you can hire an electrician to rough in new wiring, then do the final fixture connections yourself.

Some kinds of wiring require professional attention before new fixtures can be installed. An old home with wiring from before the 1920s may have a knob and tube wiring system, identifiable by paper-coated wires routed through porcelain insulating brackets and sleeves (photo lower right). Some homes built in the 1960s and 1970s may still have aluminum wiring, identifiable by its silver color and the AL stamp on receptacles and cable

Stripping NM cable sheathing

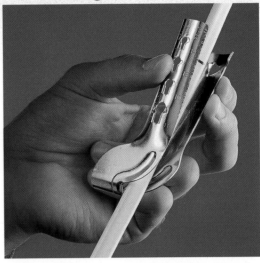

Measure and cut a length of NM cable. At each end of the cable, use a cable ripper to remove 10" of sheathing. Slide the ripper onto the cable so that the cutting point is 10" from the cable end. Squeeze the ripper so the cutting point pierces the sheathing. Pull the ripper toward the end of the cable. Peel back the cut sheathing and paper wrapping and trim them away with a utility knife or combination tool.

sheathing. Aluminum wiring must not be used with receptacles and switches intended for copper wiring. Both knob and tube and aluminum wiring represent potential fire hazards and should be inspected by a professional before you make any installations.

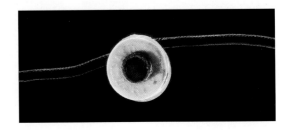

DRAWING POWER FROM AN EXISTING RECEPTACLE

One way to get power to a new fixture in a new location is by drawing power from a nearby receptacle.

1. First, shut off the power to the receptacle. Remove the receptacle from the box by unscrewing the mounting screws and carefully pulling it out of the box. Test the receptacle with a neon tester to make sure that the power is off. Undo the terminal screws on the receptacle and set the receptacle aside. Remove a knockout from the box.

Run a cable to the receptacle from the new switch or fixture. Thread the cable through the knockout, and secure it with a cable clamp, leaving 11" extra for making connections. Remove 10½" of sheathing from the cable and ¾" of insulation from each of the wires.

2. Using a wire connector, connect the white circuit wire from the old cable, the white wire of the new cable, and one end of a short piece of white insulated 12-gauge wire (called a pigtail). Then, connect the other end of the pigtail to the silver (neutral) terminal on the receptacle. Connect the black circuit wires from the new and old cable to a black pigtail, and then connect the pigtail to the brass (hot) terminal. Use a green or bare pigtail to connect the grounding circuit wires to the grounding screw on the receptacle. Tuck the wires and the receptacle back in the box and replace the mounting screws. Install the new fixture.

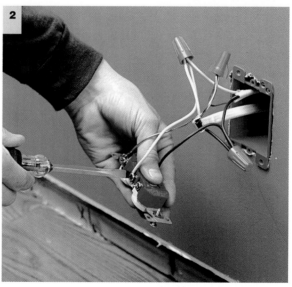

131

RUNNING CABLE ALONG A BASEBOARD

You can run cable from a receptacle to new wall or ceiling fixtures without removing much drywall by running the cable behind the baseboard.

1. Remove the baseboard between the new fixture location and the receptacle. Cut away the wall material about 1" below the top of the baseboard with a jig saw, wallboard saw, or utility knife.

2. Drill a ⅝" hole in the center of each stud between the receptacle and the fixture. A drill bit extender will allow you a better angle and make drilling the holes easier.

3. Run cable through the holes in the studs. Once you've run the cable to the stud channel where the new fixture will be located, use a fishtape to pull the cable up to the fixture box or switch box. After having your work inspected, patch the wall material, and reattach the baseboard by nailing it to the sole plate. Be careful not to nail into the studs.

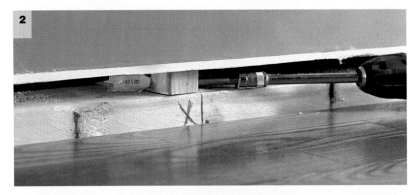

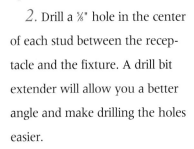

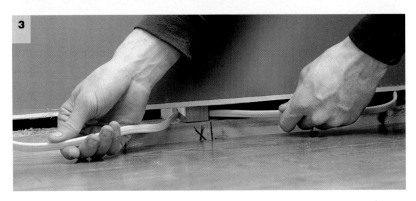

132

Running Cable into a Finished Ceiling

If you don't have access to a ceiling from above or don't have a receptacle from which to draw power, you can run cable from a receptacle in the room up the wall and into the ceiling without disturbing much of the ceiling.

1. Run cable from the receptacle along the baseboard if neccessary (see facing page) to the stud channel that aligns with the ceiling joists on which you want to install a fixture. Be sure to plan a location for the new switch.

2. Remove short strips of drywall from the wall and ceiling as shown in the illustration below. Make a notch in the center of the top plates, and protect the notch with metal nail stops.

3. Run a fish tape from the hole in the top of the wall down the wall cavity to the receptacle or baseboard channel. Pull a new cable up through the hole in the wall. Run the fish tape from the hole for the new fixture through the notch in the top plates. Pull the new cable the rest of the way to the fixture hole. After having your work inspected, replace the drywall and install the fixture and switch.

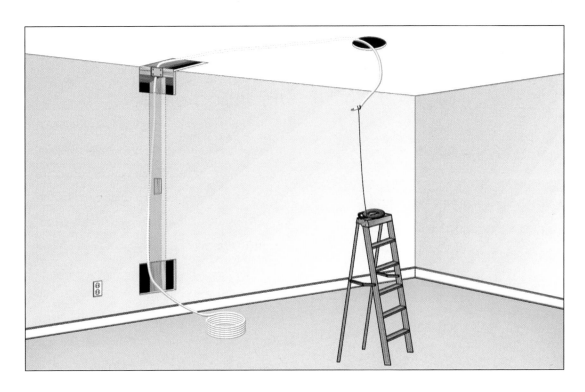

ELECTRICAL BOXES

Installing electrical boxes

All electrical codes require some sort of electrical box wherever connections and splices will be made, so if you are installing a new fixture, chances are you'll need to add a box of some kind. A huge variety of boxes is available for all sorts of indoor and outdoor switches, receptacles, and fixtures. Pick a box that fits your fixture and the type of installation. Standard metal and plastic boxes mount on the framing in the wall or ceiling. For adding fixtures and switches without disturbing the drywall, use remodeling boxes, which mount flush to the surface of the drywall. For installing fixtures between studs in walls and ceilings, boxes with built-in adjustable bracing can be installed without removing additional drywall. Whatever the installation, choose the deepest box that will fit in the wall or ceiling. Electrical connections are much easier to make if you have ample room. Talk to an electrician if you need help choosing a box for your project.

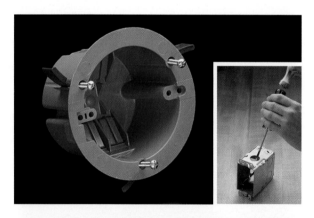

Installing fixtures on boxes

Electrical boxes have holes to accept screws for mounting plates and fixture covers. When choosing electrical boxes for new light fixtures, consult the manufacturer's recommendations. Be sure a new box will accept the weight and mounting hardware of the new fixture.

Installing cable

Electrical boxes have several knockouts—removable plastic or metal discs—where cable can enter. Use a hammer and a screwdriver to remove a knockout for each cable entering the box. To secure cable in the box, attach a cable clamp to the end of the cable and secure it in the knockout. (Some boxes have built-in clamps.) Always route at least 10" of extra cable into the box for making connections. When removing the sheathing from the cable, be sure to stop at least ½" short of the clamp.

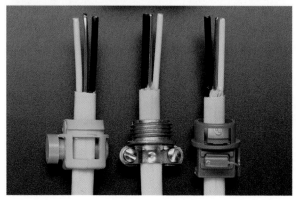

INSTALLING SINGLE-POLE SWITCHES

A single-pole switch or dimmer is the most common type of switch. It has on-off markings on the switch lever. A single-pole switch has two screw terminals and a grounding screw.

To install a single-pole switch, a hot circuit wire is attached to each screw terminal, and the neutral wires are joined together with a wire connector. However, the color and number of wires inside the switch box vary, depending on the switch's location along the electrical circuit.

1. If two cables enter the box, the switch lies between the power source and the light fixture. In this installation, attach both of the hot wires to the switch. The white circuit wires are joined together with a connector. The grounding screw on the switch is connected to the two circuit grounding wires with a short length of bare copper wire, called a *pigtail*, and a connector.

2. If only one cable enters the box, the switch lies at the end of the cable run, with the light fixture between it and the power source. In this installation (sometimes called a switch loop), attach the hot black wire to one of the screw terminals. The white wire is also hot. Code the white hot wire with black tape or paint and attach it to the other terminal. Connect the grounding circuit wire to the grounding terminal on the switch.

Once the switch is wired, tuck the wires back into the box and attach the switch to the box with screws. Restore the power and test the switch. Install a cover plate.

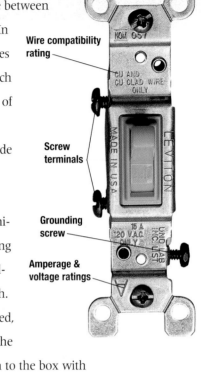

Wire compatibility rating

Screw terminals

Grounding screw

Amperage & voltage ratings

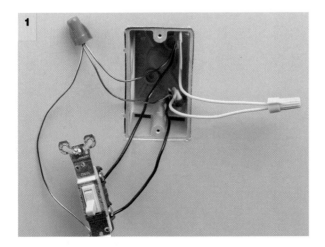

1

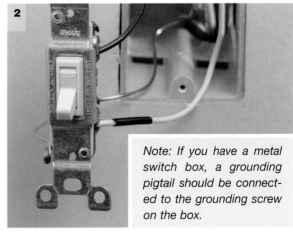

2

Note: If you have a metal switch box, a grounding pigtail should be connected to the grounding screw on the box.

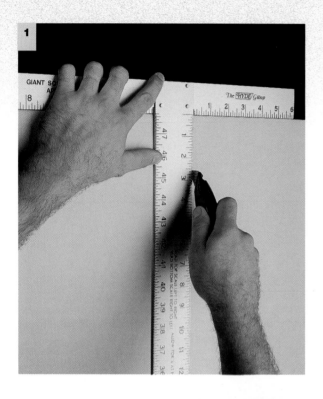

How to Install & Finish Drywall

Many light fixtures appear difficult and too time consuming to install, not because the wiring is complicated or difficult, but because they require removing and replacing drywall. Replacing sections of drywall after installing new electrical boxes is not difficult, though, and requires only a few simple tools.

Tools: *Drywall saw, utility knife, drill, 6" and 12" drywall knives.*

1. Cut a strip of drywall to fit in the opening. Use a straightedge and a utility knife to make cuts. To mark the holes in the drywall for the boxes, coat the edges of the electrical box with

chalk or lipstick and press the strip of drywall over the opening (it's easiest to do this before you've run the cable). Cut the hole with a drywall saw or utility knife.

2. Install cut panels of wallboard over the unfinished area. Anchor the panels to the framing with 1¼" wallboard screws, spaced every 10". The screw heads should be sunk just below the surface, creating a slight depression in the paper without breaking through it.

3. Apply a thin layer of wallboard joint compound over the joints and all exposed screw heads with a 4" or 6" wallboard knife. Load the knife by dipping it into a wallboard mud pan filled with joint compound.

4. Press the wallboard tape into the compound immediately, centering the tape over the joint. Smooth over the tape firmly with the 6" wallboard knife to flatten the tape and squeeze out excess compound from behind it. Let the compound dry completely.

5. Apply two thin finish coats of joint compound to the joints with a 10" or 12" wallboard knife and to the screw heads with a 4" or 6" wallboard knife. Allow the second coat to dry and shrink overnight before applying the final coat. Let the final coat dry completely before sanding. Refinish the wall and install the fixtures.

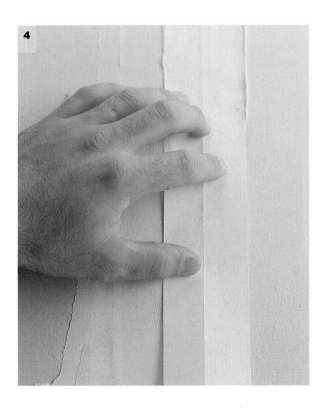

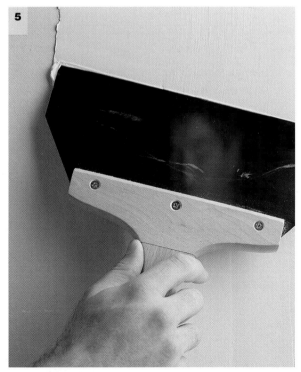

Resources

Lighting Designers

American Lighting Association
www.americanlightingassoc.com

International Association of Lighting Designers
www.iald.org

Lighting Design Lab
www.lightingdesignlab.com

Selected Manufacturers

INDOOR FIXTURES

Artemide (Italian-designed lamps and fixtures)
www.artemide.com

Eurofase (low-voltage cable kits under the brand name EasyLite)
www.eurofase.com

Flexilight
(low- and line-voltage rope lighting, including colored lights and "super-bright" versions)
www.ropelight.net

Flos
(Italian-designed lamps and fixtures)
www.flos.net

Hubbardton Forge
(handmade iron lamps and fixtures)
www.vtforge.com

Juno Lighting (recessed lighting)
www.junolighting.com

Luminaria
(period and reproduction fixtures and lamps)
www.luminaria.com

Tech Lighting (low-voltage lighting)
www.techlighting.com

WAC Lighting (low-voltage recessed lighting)
www.waclighting.com

OUTDOOR FIXTURES

Arroyo Craftsman (designer outdoor and landscape fixtures)
www.arroyo-craftsman.com

Intermatic/Malibu (low-voltage landscape fixtures and transformers)
www.intermatic.com

Kerr Lighting (recessed fixtures for decks, patios, and retaining walls)
www.kerrlighting.com

Kichler Lighting
www.kichler.com

Selected Retailers

IKEA
www.ikea.com

Illuminations
www.illuminations.com

LightingUniverse.Com
www.lightinguniverse.com

Outwater Plastics Industries, Inc.
(wide selection of low-voltage fixtures and parts, under-cabinet lighting, and rope lighting)
www.outwater.com

Room & Board
www.roomandboard.com

TerraDek Lighting
www.terradek.com

LAMP MAKING SUPPLIES

Chandelier Parts Company
www.chandelierparts.com

The Lamp Shop
www.lampshop.com

National Artcraft
www.nationalartcraft.com (sells metal candle cups for converting chandeliers)

Photo Courtesy of IKEA Home Furnishings

Contributors

Andersen Windows
800-426-4261
www.andersenwindows.com

Expanko Cork Company, Inc.
800-345-6202
www.expanko.com

Hubbardton Forge
802-468-5516
www.vtforge.com

IKEA Home Furnishings
800-434-IKEA
www.ikea.com

Illuminations
1-800-CANDLES
www.illuminations.com

Intermatic Malibu Outdoor Lighting
815-675-2321
www.intermatic.com

Kerr Lighting
613-283-9571 ext. 23
www.kerrlighting.com

Lindal Cedar Homes, Inc., Seattle, Washington
800-426-0536
www.lindal.com

Luminaria Lighting
800-638-5619
www.luminaria.com

Lutron Electronics Company, Inc.
800-523-9466
www.lutron.com

MIRAGE Prefinished Hardwood Floors
418-227-1181
www.boa-franc.com

Room & Board
800-486-6554
www.roomandboard.com

Simpson Door
800-952-6554
www.simpsondoor.com

Tech Lighting
847-410-4400
www.techlighting.com

The following photos are courtsey of Tech Lighting:

Photographer: Les Boschke
Lighting Designer: Bruce Yarnel

location - Butcher residence - Chicago, IL: p. 49

Photographer: Les Boschke
Decorative Painting: Celeste Coughlin, Asterisk
Designer: Aaron Mobarak
location - Adeline's room - Chicago, IL: p. 51

Photographer: Les Boschke
Designer: Gregory Kay
location - Kay residence - Chicago, IL: p. 76

Photographer: Les Boschke
Decorative Painting: Celeste Coughlin, Asterisk
Designer: Aaron Mobarak
location - Adeline's room - Chicago, IL: p. 90

Photographers

Beateworks, Inc.
Los Angeles, CA
www.beateworks.com

©Henry Cabala/Beateworks.com: pp. 69, 73 (bottom right)
©Christopher Covey/Beateworks.com: p. 75 (top left)
©Bill Geddes/Beateworks.com: pp. 12 (right), 27 (bottom), 52 (top), 70 (bottom right)
©Douglas Hill/Beateworks.com: p. 55 (bottom right)
©Brad Simmons/Beateworks.com: pp. 49 (bottom left), 56 (bottom), 91 (bottom)
©Tim Street-Porter/Beateworks.com: pp. 23 (both), 70 (bottom left), 72 (bottom right), 75 (top right), 77 (top right)
©Inside/Beateworks.com: pp. 33, 44, 45 (bottom), 51 (bottom)
©Amiand/Inside/Beateworks.com: p. 88 (bottom left)
©Anton/Inside/Beateworks.com: pp. 25, 111 (top)
©Baasch/Inside/Beateworks.com: pp. 30 (top), 52 (bottom)
©Claessens/Inside/Beateworks.com: p. 57(bottom left)
©De Villiers/Inside/Beateworks.com: pp. 30 (bottom), 38
©Dook/Inside/Beateworks.com: pp. 54 (bottom right), 88 (top)
© Green/Inside/Beateworks.com: pp. 34, 70 (top), 88 (bottom right)

©Millet/Inside/Beateworks.com: p. 31 (top)
©Palisse/Inside/Beateworks.com: p. 76 (bottom left)
©Raevens/Inside/Beateworks.com: p. 56 (top)
©Rodier/Inside/Beateworks.com: p. 50 (bottom)
©Saillet/Inside/Beateworks.com: p. 53 (left)
©Sarramon/Inside/Beateworks.com: p. 28
©Scotto/Inside/Beateworks.com: p. 91 (top right)
©T'Sas/Inside/Beateworks.com: pp. 12 (left), 32, 55 (bottom left), 57 (top), 71 (bottom left), 104 (bottom right)
©Vorillon/Inside/Beateworks.com: p. 43 (top)
©Wauman/Inside/Beateworks.com: p. 57 (bottom right)

Corbis
www.corbis.com
©Thomas A. Heinz/Corbis: p. 74 (top)

Getty Images
www.gettyimages.com
©Getty Images/David Toase: p. 76 (top)

Karen Melvin
Minneapolis, MN
©Karen Melvin for the following: Eric Odor, Sala Architects: p. 4; Room and Board: p. 7; Randall Buffie: p. 20; Karen Melvin—designer, Leap Day Productions—Susan Lynn, artist: p. 87; Linda Coffey—designer: p. 102-103

Image Stock Imagery, Inc.
www.indexstock.com
©Index Stock Imagery,Inc./Ted Wilcox: p. 27 (top)

©Index Stock Imagery ,Inc./Image Finders: p. 74 (bottom)

William P. Steele
New York, New York
©William P. Steele p. 48 (top left)

Veer
www.veer.com
©Salem Krieger/SolusImages p. 90 (bottom)

Jessie Walker
Glencoe, IL
©Jessie Walker pp. 53 (bottom right), 73 (bottom left)

Index

REFERENCE CHARTS

Converting Measurements

To Convert:	To:	Multiply by:
Inches	Millimeters	25.4
Inches	Centimeters	2.54
Feet	Meters	0.305
Yards	Meters	0.914
Square inches	Square centimeters	6.45
Square feet	Square meters	0.093
Square yards	Square meters	0.836
Cubic inches	Cubic centimeters	16.4
Cubic feet	Cubic meters	0.0283
Cubic yards	Cubic meters	0.765
Ounces	Milliliters	30.0
Pints (U.S.)	Liters	0.473 (Imp. 0.568)
Quarts (U.S.)	Liters	0.946 (Imp. 1.136)
Gallons (U.S.)	Liters	3.785 (Imp. 4.546)
Ounces	Grams	28.4
Pounds	Kilograms	0.454

To Convert:	To:	Multiply by:
Millimeters	Inches	0.039
Centimeters	Inches	0.394
Meters	Feet	3.28
Meters	Yards	1.09
Square centimeters	Square inches	0.155
Square meters	Square feet	10.8
Square meters	Square yards	1.2
Cubic centimeters	Cubic inches	0.061
Cubic meters	Cubic feet	35.3
Cubic meters	Cubic yards	1.31
Milliliters	Ounces	.033
Liters	Pints (U.S.)	2.114 (Imp. 1.76)
Liters	Quarts (U.S.)	1.057 (Imp. 0.88)
Liters	Gallons (U.S.)	0.264 (Imp. 0.22)
Grams	Ounces	0.035
Kilograms	Pounds	2.2

Also from

CREATIVE PUBLISHING INTERNATIONAL

Garden Style

Garden Style is the art of decorating your home with the themes, colors, textures and patterns found in the world of the living garden. This book includes two dozen step-by-step projects to help you achieve this popular decorating style in your own home.

ISBN 1-58923-007-8

Cottage Style

Cottage-style decorating seeks to recreate the romantic ambience of a rural English cottage in your home. A cottage-style home is quaint and colorful, and includes furniture and accessories chosen for their homespun charm.

ISBN 1-58923-057-4

Flea Market Style

Flea Market Style features hundreds of ideas for transforming flea market finds into reclaimed treasure. This book gives readers complete instructions for creating dozens of simple but ingenious projects.

ISBN 1-58923-000-0

Cabin Style

Cabin-style shows you how to bring the look and atmosphere of cabin living into your home. More than a decorating book, *Cabin Style* is also an introduction to a simpler, more relaxed way of living, along with step-by-step directions for nearly two dozen projects.

ISBN 1-58923-058-2

CREATIVE PUBLISHING INTERNATIONAL

18705 LAKE DRIVE EAST
CHANHASSEN, MN 55317

WWW.CREATIVEPUB.COM